Framework for the Curriculum

MONOGRAPH No. 2

FRAMEWORK FOR THE CURRICULUM

Monographs in Curriculum Studies

General Editor : Philip H. Taylor

in association with :

Ann Hurman
Penelope Weston

Supported in part by an SSRC Grant

Framework for the Curriculum

A Study in Secondary Schooling

Penelope B. Weston

NFER Publishing Company Ltd

Published by the NFER Publishing Company Ltd.,
Darville House, 2 Oxford Road East, Windsor, Berks. SL4 1DF
Registered Office: The Mere, Upton Park, Slough, Berks. SL1 2DQ
First published 1977

© *P. H. Taylor and P. B. Weston 1977*
This report was produced with a grant from the Social Science Research
Council for selected studies in curriculum theory
ISBN 0 85633 137 6

Typeset by Jubal Multiwrite Ltd., 66 Loampit Vale, London SE13 7SN
Printed in Great Britain by
Whitefriars Press, Medway Wharf Road, Tonbridge, Kent
Distributed in the USA by Humanities Press Inc.,
Atlantic Highlands, New Jersey 07716 USA.

To Simon, Vicki and Lucy

who will all reach the third year before too long

Contents

TABLES AND FIGURES

FOREWORD AND ACKNOWLEDGEMENTS

The 13—14 Curriculum Study formed part of a research programme financed by the Social Science Research Council for a period of five years. The main aim of the study was to discover and describe what happens in the 'third year': what is taught; to whom; with what emphases; in what circumstances, and to study the data obtained in order to make judgments about the 'official' and 'hidden' curricula, their interactions and their joint effects on the education of pupils. The 13—14 age-range was chosen for a variety of reasons: first, the research team wanted to confine the study to secondary schools, and this is the youngest group who will certainly be in secondary schools whatever the age of entry; second, it seemed to us that it is generally in the 11—14 age-range that the secondary school has the fullest opportunity for shaping and defining its own curriculum; third, the third year is usually the year in which pupils are invited to make choices about their courses for the fourth and fifth years and it seemed important to look in detail at this decision-making period.

The study was divided into two stages. During Stage One the research team gathered general information from a sample of 117 West Midlands schools. This was done via three questionnaires: the first asking for basic information about schools' size, age-range, accommodation, and so on; the second dealing with details of the third year timetable and the way in which pupils were grouped and re-grouped across the curriculum; and a third, inquiring into teacher attitudes towards the curriculum. In addition, a Pupil Opinion Questionnaire was piloted and developed for use later in the study. An analysis of the information from these questionnaires enabled us to shape the second stage work, in which we aimed to look more clearly at the third year curriculum in a smaller number of schools. At the beginning of Stage Two, a pilot study, mainly to test a variety of research methods, was carried out in two schools not in the main sample. This stage was then finally planned to have two parts: detailed case studies in two schools and, alongside that, 'background studies' via questionnaires and some visits, in 18 schools — all carefully chosen to be as representative as possible of the main sample.

This book is one of a series which is intended to cover a number of different aspects of the study — the option system and how it operates; what is taught in English and Science and Art; what teachers and some pupils believe to be the purposes of schooling; and the subjects that are taught.

This study has been a team effort: the research staff, the advisory groups and all the schools who have taken part. All those individuals or groups who have participated in any official way in the study — and there are many of them — are listed at the end of this book. We on the research staff owe a large debt of gratitude to all those who have given their time and energy to help with the study over the last four years and, indeed, to make it possible at all.

For my own part, I must also thank those who have helped me at various stages with the work for this book, particularly my colleagues in the Faculty of Education: Robert Lambourne, for patient advice on computing problems; Roy Lowe and David Rolf for valuable advice on the historical issues; and Bill Reid for good ideas and much encouragement. I am grateful, too, to Denise Plumpton, who was then a student at Sheffield University, for many diligent hours and much skilful assistance with the computer work. And I want to thank, however inadequately, my immediate colleagues for their support and help: the Study's director, Philip Taylor; Ann Hurman, without whom the manuscript would never have reached a final draft; Andrea Scarboro; and Irene Godfrey and Sally Ginns who patiently transformed the drafts into a finished typescript. Finally, I would like to thank my family for learning to live with the curriculum.

Explanatory note on curriculum pattern diagrams

In many large schools, the curriculum and the timetable that represents the detailed operation of the curriculum is a complex affair, covering a large sheet of paper and taking some time to describe in words. For this reason I have adopted the shorthand of the curriculum pattern diagram, as used in Davies (1969) and elsewhere. An example is given below:

name of class	number of pupils in class	subjects taught to each class as a single group	subjects for which classes are combined and regrouped
3A	31	E_5 M_5 F_4 P_2 Ch_2 B_2 G_3 H_3 RE_1 Mu_1	$A/A/A_2$
3B	29	E_5 M_5 F_4 P_2 Ch_2 B_2 G_3 H_3 RE_1 Mu_1	Nk/Mk_3
			HE/Wk_3
		('E_5' = English, 5 periods)	$PE/PE/_2$
			Ga/Ga_2

This format makes it possible to describe concisely the subjects offered, the time allotted to them and the arrangements made for different groups of pupils. But its use is limited; it shows, for instance, when pupils are taught in their basic teaching groups and when they are regrouped with other pupils, but not the method of grouping used — whether it is by sex, specific ability or pupil choice, for example. Most of the subject abbreviations are probably self-explanatory, but a full list is given in Appendix C.

INTRODUCTION

'Since I've not had much formal education, I've had to use my brains.'

Bill Shankly, Liverpool FC Manager in a
television interview, September 1976.

In these days secondary schools and the education that goes on in them convey a formal and even forbidding image to many outsiders: either it is all highly structured, or (if the media are to be believed) anarchy prevails because the structures have broken down. Many large schools do seem very complex and even bureaucratic in their organization, although in some cases a sophisticated organizational approach can result in simple and flexible patterns. But head teachers would probably all agree that the structures are never more than a means to an end and that end could be summed up succinctly as helping *all* children to learn to use their brains. In everyday terms, it may be the teacher in the classroom who is the most important exponent of this aim, but it is the general theme of this book that the framework in which the learning process goes on will play an important part in shaping the curriculum, particularly in the complex structures of most secondary schools. In this study, the idea is worked out in relation to the third year curriculum in one sample of secondary schools.

When the schools were invited to participate in Stage One of the 13—14 Curriculum Study the intention was to include as wide a variety of secondary schools as could be found within a limited geographical area. Early in 1974 invitations were sent to all maintained secondary schools in seven local education authorities (LEAs) in the Midlands area, and to the direct grant and independent schools in these areas with pupils in the 13—14 age range. In all, 70 per cent of those invited agreed to take part, although a slightly smaller number (100 schools) completed both the Stage One questionnaires. Information obtained from these questionnaires showed that the sample proved to be reasonably typical of secondary schools in England and Wales as a whole, as described in national statistics,[1] in terms of school types (grammar, secondary modern, comprehensive), the sex of the pupils, and the age, sex and qualifications of the staff within the schools. There were schools with different ages of entry (65 per cent had an entry at 11+ or under, 26 per cent at 12+, and 9 per cent at 13+), and of leaving: 61 per cent had sixth forms, but schools in some areas were linked with sixth-form colleges or sixth forms in other schools, and all pupils therefore left at 16. The schools varied widely in size, both in the

total number of pupils and the size of the third year group: although
the mean figure for the year groups was 154 pupils, 50 per cent of
schools had 140 or fewer, and there was a small group of schools —
about 10 per cent of the total — which had year groups of 300 or more.
There were marked differences, too, in sites, buildings and resources,
from cramped city sites with difficult old buildings, to new, spacious
purpose-built premises with extensive specialist facilities, or a school in
a rural setting with good opportunities for environmental studies. Some
schools were in Educational Priority Areas with small, densely
populated catchment zones, while a few were primarily boarding
schools, drawing their pupils from all over the country and abroad.

All these facts and figures, however, relate to the circumstances of
1974, and already change was the order of the day; 67 per cent of the
schools had experienced some degree of reorganization from without in
the previous five years (1969—74), and another 14 per cent were facing
imminent change. By 1976, with the ending of 11+ selection in some
more areas and the changes that followed on local government
reorganization in 1974, the outward circumstances of some schools had
changed radically — in one instance from a girls' grammar school
directly to a mixed 11—16 comprehensive school.[2] In this sense, too,
the sample may be considered typical, including as it did some
authorities which already had a stable and reasonably uniform pattern
of comprehensive schools, some which retained 11+ selection and
others which were enmeshed in the complexities of institutional
change.

In order to study the third year curriculum in greater detail in Stage
Two, we needed to approach a smaller number of schools, but it was
important that these should represent as far as possible the variety
found in the larger group.[3] The head teachers of 25 of the original 117
schools were asked if they would continue with Stage Two of the
study. Eighteen of these felt able to cooperate fully, and it was in these
schools that the 'background studies' relating to the third year
curriculum were carried out. The schools were asked to supply
timetables, curriculum outlines, handbooks and other general
information, and to make more detailed returns for the three subjects
chosen for special study — English, Art and Science. The two case study
schools (also chosen from the original sample) were both mixed
comprehensive schools with over one thousand pupils. In these schools
two members of the research team made a close study of the third year
curriculum, talking to teachers and pupils observing lessons and trying
to monitor any activities which earlier investigations had suggested were
important for an understanding of the third year.

This book, which is concerned with the framework that sustains and
defines the curriculum in the school, draws upon material from both

stages of the study, as well as other evidence, particularly aspects of recent English educational history which are considered in Part I. Analysis of data from the second of the Stage One surveys, the Timetable Questionnaire, forms the basis of Part II, and in Part III material from the eighteen 'background studies' schools and the two case study schools is used to present a rather more detailed account of the shape of the third year curriculum and to describe some of the factors which may have influenced this.

Some of the issues discussed in this book could have arisen from a general study of the secondary school curriculum; how the school day is divided up, how far schools are concerned with teaching separate subjects or integrated programmes, what types of pupil grouping are favoured in which schools; but by focussing on a particular age group, as we have done in this study, these general issues can be considered in a much more closely defined context, and in addition certain questions will emerge which are specific to that age group or become of particular concern at that stage — like, for example, the question of whether of how choices should be made for fourth year courses.

There is an interesting juxtaposition of the predictable and the problematic in the study of the third year curriculum. In a 'normal' five year secondary school course the third year marks the halfway point, an in-between stage, with the generalized enthusiasm of the lower school behind and the new challenge of examination or 'leavers' courses ahead. 'Everyone knows' what pupils study at this stage — they follow a general course whose outlines are familiar to all teachers — there is surely little here that is controversial, and so what can this study really be about? — as we have often been asked. And yet, partly because of the English educational inheritance, when one digs a little below the surface there is diversity at almost every level: in the size and type of institutions in which fourteen-year-old pupils are to be found, in the internal organization of the school, in the experience and expectations which pupils and teachers bring with them, in the later courses for which this third year is a foundation, and, of course, at the level of the third year classroom itself. Some of the reasons for this diversity lie in the past, in the way in which the present patchwork of secondary provision has evolved from the two main traditions of post-primary schooling that have existed for much of the century. It is for this reason that I have attempted in Part I of the book to trace how the age group has fared during the last seventy years, and what sort of curriculum (or curricula) they have experienced. There have been marked changes in the school context for this age group; only for the last thirty years have all fourteen-year-olds been in school at all, and for the majority before this date the 13–14 curriculum wavered between vocational pressures and the desire to equip all pupils with a general education that would broaden their horizons and instil into as many as possible a desire for life-long education. Only in the grammar schools, as they were called after 1944, could the needs of all third year pupils be seen clearly in the context of a five year course, and it was here that the idea of a common foundation course for all pupils, composed of a collection of recognized subjects or disciplines, grew up — a course that was planned at first for two and then for three years. But when this approach was adopted in the early post-war comprehensive schools, the old bipartite tradition and the custom of grouping pupils according to 'general ability' quickly invested the concept of a common course for all pupils with controversial overtones — variations on the meaning of equality. And even if all pupils could usefully follow a common course when they arrived at their (common) secondary school at eleven, was it not essential to provide in the formal curriculum for a variety of needs by the age of 14, especially when the diverse educational futures of pupils were considered? As one head teacher remarked:[4]

> 'The third year curriculum is inevitably a compromise. Conflict between a common curriculum with stable primary groups and increased specialization with the flexibility required is most acute in the third year.'

In Part I, then, a historical context is established for some of the issues which became familiar as we made our study of the third year curriculum. Of these, the meaning and significance of this concept of the common course is one of the most salient. Is it a common course if some pupils take a second or third language? If the same subjects are studied by all but for different lengths of time? If pupils are in upper, middle and lower bands or streams? If boys and girls take different subjects? Do any schools reject the aim of a common course at this stage in favour of individual choice, or 'tracks' with clearly differentiated courses? In Part II these questions are discussed and some answers suggested by looking at what the practice was in the whole sample of schools which participated in Stage One. Schools had been asked to describe the context of the third year curriculum in some detail; how the timetable was structured in terms of units of time and the length of the cycle; the basic pattern of the curriculum (a common or differentiated course), and its content (what subjects were taught); the way pupils were grouped in the third year; and the main obstacles that seemed to prevent teachers from carrying out their cherished plans and aims. The replies given by the schools showed that there was much common ground. It became clear, for example that most schools were operating a curriculum that was conventional in outward appearance; familiar subject names appeared on nearly all timetables, with only a sprinkling of integrated humanities courses or design programmes. But although most schools described their third year curriculum as a common course (with some exceptions, usually related to languages), it was very often arranged for classes grouped for much of the time according to ability. And it seemed that differences over grouping were as much a matter of principle as pragmatism; in their ideal world, some head teachers would change to mixed ability classes, but equally some yearned for more setting and homogeneous groups.

The data obtained from the questionnaire suggested trends and described outlines. The material that has been used in Part III, from the Stage Two schools, enabled us to look more closely at the third year curriculum. With the two case study schools one could begin from within a context that had become very familiar. It was possible to set the third year pattern into the context of the whole school curriculum, and to look back in time to see how this pattern had developed, in both cases in schools which, in their different ways, had 'gone comprehensive' within the last ten years. In this respect they may stand for a great number of secondary schools, even though in so many ways each school is unique. The structure and outline of the third year curriculum in these two schools could then be set against findings from the wider group of eighteen schools, and common issues discussed.

Most of this book is concerned with description; looking at the third year and the framework of their curriculum from several angles to try to build up a picture of 'how it is'. Some suggestions are offered along the way about how it has come to be so; then in Part IV, by contrast, the aim is to review the evidence and look at possible trends as the period of institutional change and expansion in secondary schools is transformed into a time of contraction and cutback.

NOTES

1. For example, *Statistics of Education 1972, Vols I and II*. Department of Education and Science, (1973) and *SSI Survey of the curriculum and deployment of teachers (Secondary Schools) 1965—6, Part I: Teachers*. Department of Education and Science, (1971).
2. See page 28 for some further examples of these changes.
3. For details of how these schools were selected, see Appendix A.
4. See also pages 82—83 for the context of this comment.

PART I

Historical Background: 13–14: Third Year Pupils and their Curriculum, 1900–1977

Introductory

'The secondary school timetable is a structure that portrays the curriculum organization of a school: the completed timetable reveals the school's curriculum policy . . .

It is like it is, not necessarily because it achieves for the pupils the educational encounters that are appropriate to their needs and interests, but for reasons which precede the actual timetable that is put on the Common Room notice board by many years. Any consideration of present-day timetables and the value judgments associated with their construction must take into account this history.'[1]

As Walton suggests here, in his useful historical introduction to a collection of studies on *The Secondary School Timetable* it is impossible to separate 'timetable' and 'curriculum', since any timetable is only a particular representation of 'curriculum policy'. But how much can be deduced about that policy from any 'particular representation' that one may be faced with? As Davies (1969) points out when describing the task of the new headmaster on taking over a school:

'Of one thing we can be absolutely certain: he is the inheritor of a curriculum that is set out in detail in the school timetable that hangs on the wall of his room.'[2]

That this may be almost all he has from which to deduce the 'curriculum policy' of his new school is underlined by evidence from our own 13—14 Study. During an interview, one headmaster was asked whether, when he took up office, the existing pattern of the curriculum in the school was clear to him:

'No, it wasn't clear when I came. I had a timetable — full stop. Plus a brief, describing the whole school, on two sides of foolscap, that was given to me when I applied for the post.'

In seeking to understand this timetable, to put flesh on its bare bones, the headmaster or any newcomer will find it necessary to get immersed in all the complex detail of the school — its staff, pupils, buildings and resources. But almost inevitably he will be drawn to ask questions about how some particular feature came to assume its present shape. This uncovering of the history of a school's curricular policy may prove at least as valuable, in planning for growth and development, as the received wisdom of the school management course.

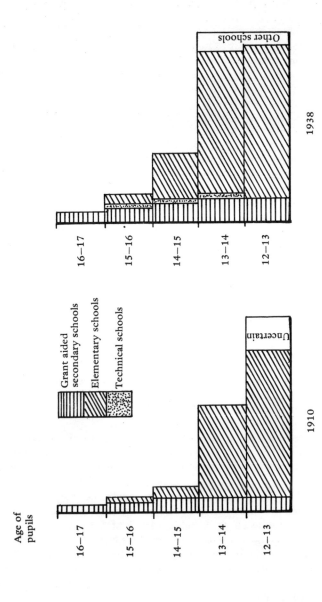

Figure 1.1: Secondary age population in England and Wales, 1910–1974: percentage in various types of school.

Figure 1 cont'd

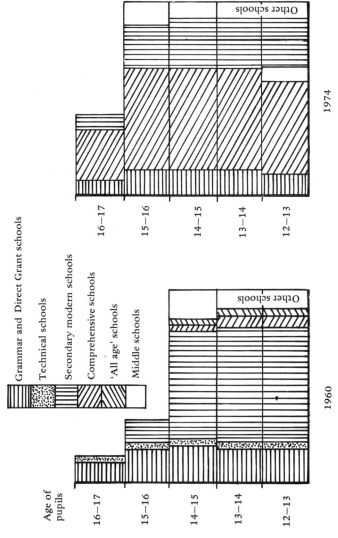

Age of
pupils

Grammar and Direct Grant schools

Technical schools

Secondary modern schools

Comprehensive schools

'All age' schools

Middle schools

16—17

15—16

14—15

13—14

12—13

Other schools

1960

16—17

15—16

14—15

13—14

12—13

Other schools

1974

This book is concerned with timetables, and other organizational matters, insofar as this provides a framework for the third year curriculum. If *particular* timetables and the curricula they embody are shaped in important ways by their history, as Davies suggests, it seems valuable to explore from a historical perspective how the curriculum for this age-group developed. But the 13—14 age group cannot be understood in isolation and it is necessary first to establish their place in the school context over the years.

1. The 13—14 age group in the public educational system 1900—1977

During the present century the place of the 13—14 age group in the school system as a whole (in England and Wales) has changed gradually but radically. In 1910 (as shown in Figure 1.1), the only group of pupils over thirteen in the maintained system who had a clear obligation to remain in school were those in the newly defined[3] secondary schools, for whom an 11/12 — 16 (or 18) course was planned. True, a considerable number of pupils remained in the higher classes of the elementary schools, or the new Central Schools, but with the elementary school leaving age standing at thirteen,* educational provision for older pupils was at best haphazard. Even in 1917, one year before the Education Act which set the leaving age at fourteen, it was estimated in the Lewis Report[4] that between 20 and 25 per cent of all children aged 13—14 were not receiving any kind of 'public educational training', and for the next age group, 14—15, this proportion rose to 70 per cent. After 1918,** there were effectively three school-leaving ages: fourteen (for the vast majority), sixteen (for many 'secondary' pupils who left after taking the new School Certificate), and eighteen for the small minority who went on to university. At the same time, a number of pupils in the 'post-primary' sector were staying on till fifteen in order to complete a vocational or technically-based general course that might lead to a better job. Although the proportion of pupils following full-time courses after their fourteenth birthdays increased markedly between the wars (see Figure 1.1) for most pupils at this period the 'third year' in our terms, was their last year in school, and according to the date of their birthday it might only be a part year at that. Moreover, it was likely to be spent in the same school where they had started their education some nine years earlier. The task of their teachers was to devise a curriculum

---

* Parents could obtain exemption from full-time education for their children if they were over twelve and had reached a satisfactory standard.

** The Education Act of 1918 fixed the leaving age at fourteen by abolishing all exemptions; because of 'economy drives' this change did not come into effect till 1922.

suitable for this terminal year of their education.

Up to the Second World War, then, the main division in terms of curriculum planning still fell between the rather precisely defined five-year course for pupils in 'secondary schools' and the miscellaneous collection of 'elements', subjects and courses variously provided by local authorities for all other pupils. But already the Hadow Committee in their report on *The Education of the Adolescent* (1926) had outlined a wholly new school system which would consider all adolescents as a single group, at least initially. They recommended that:

'It is desirable that education up to 11+ should be known by the general name of Primary Education, and education after 11 by the general name of Secondary Education.'[5]

They further recommended that existing 'Secondary' schools should be called 'Grammar Schools', and most other types of schools for the 11+ age group should be designated 'Modern Schools'. But despite the considerable influence which this report undoubtedly had on educational thinking, especially in relation to the curriculum for older pupils, many of its particular recommendations — notably the raising of the school leaving age to fifteen — were not implemented till the post-war period. Indeed, two later Reports issued by the Board of Education — the Spens Report of 1938,[6] and the Norwood Report of 1943,[7] went back over some of the same ground, particularly in relation to the organization of the secondary system. It was the Norwood Report which spelt out in detail the tripartite system which had been foreshadowed in 1926 and outlined in the Spens Report, and the Education Act of 1944 that gave it legislative reality. But it was not until the long-standing promise to raise the school leaving age to fifteen was finally realized in 1947 that the position of 'third year' pupils underwent any substantial change. Now all pupils would at least *begin* a fourth year, many would complete it, and a growing number would even consider staying an 'extra year', up to sixteen. Whereas there had been little incentive to plan the biased courses envisaged by the Hadow Committee for the years 13—15, now new thinking could begin. Loukes (1956)[8] suggests that very often this would take the form of a communal project for the fourth year, but that there was a tendency for the curriculum to change earlier, during the third year. The implications of these changes for the third year curriculum itself will be explored further below. For the moment it is only important to emphasize that the form of the educational structures still had a marked effect on the curricular horizons of 'third year' pupils. The tripartite — or as Walton (1972) describes it, 'in reality, bipartite' — system underlined the traditional pattern of separate planning, especially as the one clear official guideline for the new secondary modern schools was that they should not be restricted by the requirements of a public examination. In addition, the new (1951) General Certificate of Education (GCE) was designed, at first by regulation and then by custom, for fifth year pupils, and was therefore inappropriate for the time scale as well as the ability range of secondary modern schools as a whole.

Over the past twenty years, three factors have been mainly responsible for changing this situation. First, from 1976,* all pupils must remain at school till at least May 31 of the school year in which they become sixteen,** and therefore from an organizational point of view all *should* have the opportunity to take '16+' examinations. More generally, the raising of the school leaving age to sixteen has meant that schools *must* plan a five-year course for all their pupils, and this has had the profound effect of making the third year a time of decision and forward planning for *all* pupils. Secondly, over the period as a whole, there has been a marked change in official policy about terminal public examinations for secondary school pupils. Very soon after the introduction of the new 'single subject' GCE examination many secondary modern school teachers seized the opportunity it gave for their abler pupils to receive the accolade of public examination success, and instituted external examination forms or streams for those able pupils who would guarantee to stay on till the end of the fifth year. This trend was particularly marked in areas where 'selective' places at 11+ were only available to a small proportion of the age group.[10] In this way, the distinction between the goals of the two types of school became blurred. This policy was given some degree of official sanction in 1958 in *Secondary Education for All, a New Drive*[11] which advocated the development of advanced courses in secondary modern schools. Furthermore, it was, in part, pressure from the secondary modern schools for some form of public accreditation for the majority of their pupils that led to the setting up of the Beloe Committee whose report was published in 1958. The Certificate of Education that this Committee recommended was awarded for the first time in 1965,† amid intensive consultation and research by the newly established Schools Council. From then on, a far larger proportion of the school population has been encouraged to set its sights on some form of public examination at 16+, and this, too, has had important results for the shape and direction of the third year course. Thirdly, the upheaval of

---

* The school-leaving age was raised to sixteen in 1972, but pupils could leave at Easter if their sixteenth birthday fell before that date. This meant that a new category of non-examination candidates was created — the fifth year 'Easter leavers'.
** This ruling has created some anomalies in schools where CSE and GCE examinations continue after this date.
† In practice, it came to be called 'The Certificate of Secondary Education' (CSE).

school reorganization and the move away from 11+ selection have had far-reaching effects; particularly on the way in which work is organized within the school. With the end of differentiation by 11+ selection, the ideal of a common course for *all* pupils (which had been recommended for the first two years of the secondary course by the Spens Report in 1938) seemed a real possibility. And the greatly increased size of many of the new schools called for wholly new approaches to organization and timetabling, so that it seemed possible that the old groupings of forms and streams, which tended to perpetuate the old grammar/modern divisions within the one school, might disappear in a welter of 'primary groups', 'open sets' and 'consistent blocking'.

One further consequence of the reorganization of secondary education should be mentioned, because it bears directly on the position of third year pupils in the system as a whole. One of the most obvious and least equivocal results of the 1944 Education Act was that from then on there would be a break at 11+ for all pupils in the maintained sector between the primary and secondary stage, and for almost all this would involve a move from one school to another, whether to a grammar, technical or secondary modern school, or even to one of the new 11—18 comprehensive schools being established in London and Coventry. When the first 'high school' was established in Leicestershire in 1957, it introduced a further break *within* the secondary age range (at 14+), but did not breach the 11+ line, since the high schools were clearly regarded as 'junior secondary'. Convinced advocates of comprehensive education were beginning to look at other possible forms of organization which might be just as valid as the 11—18 school for all, which was proving so difficult to introduce in many areas. Thus when Circular 10/65 was issued (1965)[12] it was envisaged that transfer to the final stage of compulsory education might be at any age between eleven and fourteen; this had been made legally possible by the Education Act of 1964 which abolished the statutory requirement for transition to secondary education at eleven. From plans for reorganization approved by 1968, Benn and Simon (1972) could project that 25 per cent of all comprehensive schools planned would be in 'tiered' systems, with a break at thirteen or fourteen, and a number of local education authorities (including two covered by the 13—14 Study) would have comprehensive schools with a starting age of twelve.[13] If, therefore, one is concerned with the curriculum of *secondary* schools, the 'third year' (i.e. the 13—14 age group) is the youngest group of pupils who will certainly be in such a school, as distinct from a primary or middle school.* Thus whereas the changes in

---

* The only exception to this seems to be in those areas, like Leicestershire, where 10—14 middle schools have been introduced.

the circumstances of 13—14 year-olds, from 1900 to 1965 came in general 'from above', with the raising of the school leaving age and its consequences, recent changes, affecting only some pupils and less widely remarked, have come from below. In other words, the educational career of a pupil *before* he is thirteen, in terms of types of school attended, may now show as much variety as we have become accustomed to see in the later years of the secondary school. So one question to be borne in mind during this investigation concerns the differences, if any, in curricular provision for the third year which may be observed between 11+ entry schools and, say, 13+ entry schools.

2. The curriculum for the 13—14 age group: two twentieth century traditions

If the position of fourteen-year-old pupils in the educational system has undergone these changes, how has this been reflected in the content and aims of their school curriculum? First of all, it is instructive to look at the curricula of those pupils who have throughout the century been expected to follow a five year course: the grammar school group. The official curriculum for the grammar school can be traced in detail from the *Regulations for Secondary Schools* of 1904, through the Spens and Norwood reports, supplemented by the requirements made by the major examining bodies. It would be absurd to say there has been no change, but the most striking feature of this curriculum is its stability, in aims, structure and to a lesser extent, contents and methods. There are schools in many areas which still embody this tradition in a clearly recognizable form, but their number is shrinking rapidly and teachers who have worked mostly within this tradition may be faced with wholly new challenges. In the 13—14 Study, out of 117 schools there were, in 1974, seventeen maintained grammar schools and thirteen other 'selective' schools (four Direct Grant schools and nine Independent schools) which would, in general, represent this tradition. In addition there were eight schools which had been grammar schools, and still contained some 'selective' pupils, if only in the sixth form. At the time of writing (1976), of the maintained 'selective' schools, one has closed, seven have already had at least one year of comprehensive intake or have become comprehensive by merging with other schools, and two others are commencing the process in the current year (1976/77). One is becoming a sixth-form college. So there are only six of these schools still in being wholly as grammar schools and all these are in local education authority areas where, as a result of local government reorganization and the present economic climate, a mixed economy is still in operation with regard to selection and age of entry. So all but a few of these schools are in a period of transition, when their staff will be earnestly considering how best to cater for the new all-ability intake. These deliberations may be radical, going back to fundamental questions about the purpose of secondary education, or they may be more pragmatic, looking first at what has been provided hitherto for the majority who have not been selected for grammar school. This may be the natural approach in a situation where a new comprehensive school is formed by a merger, as is the case with two single-sex grammar schools in the 13—14 Study which have recently merged with two single-sex secondary modern schools. In this case there are likely to be teachers in the 'new' schools who represent both traditions and seek to preserve the best in each while being open to new ideas as well (as well as the minority who find it difficult to adjust). But how is one to identify the 'non-grammar school' tradition (to use a negative definition for the moment)? By contrast with the clear outline of that examination-defined curriculum, it seems at first a much more slippery and amorphous concept. But over the years certain strands can be identified, although the way they are combined and the curricular pattern that results, may change considerably from one period to another. The development of the two traditions for the third year curriculum, 'grammar' and 'non-grammar', is summarized in diagrammatic form in Figures 1.2 and 1.3.

Some form of commentary is needed for these diagrammatic summaries. The various headings down the side have been chosen to give some idea of the *context* in which this third year curriculum was being carried out: the length of the course, and whether it culminated in public examinations for all or most of the pupils; the type of school and some indication of the background of the teachers; the type of group or groups in which third year pupils would be likely to find themselves. Then some attempt has been made to indicate from contemporary sources the outline of the curriculum itself in terms of subjects offered and the time to be allocated to them, with, in addition, the amount of homework expected from these pupils.

This curricular cross-section has been presented for three dates spanning the century, but selected with particular factors in mind. The first, 1910, represents a point in time when the new secondary schools, ushered in by Morant after the 1902 Education Act, were settling into a recognizable pattern, while the rest of the 'post-primary' sector struggled and chafed under the restrictions of the Elementary Code. By 1940 — no allowance being made in this schematic representation for the upheaval caused by the outbreak of war and the mass evacuation of schoolchildren — there had been notable changes especially for the great majority of pupils who did not attend grammar schools. Many of the recommendations of the Hadow Committee (1926) had been put into effect by local education authorities and teachers, in the shape of reorganized senior schools (attended by 48 per cent of children in

Figure 1.2: The 'third year' curriculum in selective secondary (grammar) schools 1910–1960

	Circa 1910	circa 1940	circa 1960
TYPE OF SCHOOL	COUNTY/MUNICIPAL SECONDARY GRAMMAR/HIGH SCHOOL (grant aided)	COUNTY HIGH/GRAMMAR SCHOOL	COUNTY HIGH/GRAMMAR
CONTENT OF 'THIRD YEAR' COURSE	All pupils following 11/12 – 16 course; age of entry varies, and at 13+ pupils may be in third or fourth year of course.	Generally as 1910 but entry now usually at 11+. Spens (1938) recommended a common course for the first *two* years, and parallel but different courses for the next three.	Little major change, but 11+ entry clarified after 1944, and since all must pass 11+ exam, untested 'feepaying' pupils eliminated. Therefore third year—13/14 age-group, unless express form in being. Common course for *three* years now recommended, with some exceptions.
BACKGROUND OF TEACHERS	Mostly (64% of men, 42% of women) graduates, with or without further training. (About one-third had a recognized training).	As 1910, but more graduates (78%) and many now had one year professional training, especially at a time of job-shortage. (66% of all teachers were trained).	Mostly graduates (78% again), but some college-trained specialists. 73% of *all* graduate teachers were trained.
EXAMINATION AIMS FOR 'THIRD YEAR' PUPILS	Many possible examinations, mostly set up by independent University Examination Boards or professional bodies. Included 'Junior Certificates', to be taken at 14 or 15.	School Certificate ('First certificate'), at least *five* subjects to be taken, including one from each of three groups: English subjects (incl. Humanities), Languages other than English, Science and Maths. Also Group IV – Music, Art etc. Matriculation, which demanded higher standard in exam, came to be seen as a 'top grade' certificate.	GCE: pupils may take any number of subjects, but most will be advised to take at least seven, to include English, Maths, a science, a foreign Language, and one of the Humanities. Some may take ten or more.
TYPE OF TEACHING GROUP	Form, e.g. IVa, Vb, Shell. Age range in any form might be wide. In 'third year', a number of different subjects would still be taught by form master/mistress.	Form. 'Express form' might be selected in third year to prepare for School Certificate in fourth year. Spens report recommended streaming.	Form: parallel forms may have replaced streaming, but express form may still operate. Setting, by ability (e.g. for Maths) or by aptitude (e.g. for different crafts) is increasing, but it affects upper school more than third year.
CONTENT AND STRUCTURE OF 'THIRD YEAR' CURRICULUM	1904 'Regulations' stated the following minima for all secondary schools: English, History and Geography 4½ hours per week One foreign language 3½ } Two foreign languages* or 6 } Science and Maths 7½ (at least 3 for Science) plus instruction in Physical exercises, Drawing, Singing, Manual training (boys) or Housewifery (girls). *when two languages were taken, Latin should usually be one of them. This was seen as a general curriculum for all. The time prescriptions were omitted after 1907, but they remained a guide.	Abstract from possible grammar school timetable, 1942 (3 form entry mixed). (Walton, 1972, p. 27). School population in September approx. 428 3S = Science side, 3M = Modern side, 3T = Transitus (i.e. potential early leavers). NB. Note setting across the year group for Maths.	Possible timetable for third year, 3 form entry mixed grammar school. 3A (30) $E_5H_3G_3RE_2F_5Ger/L_4$ $B_2C_2P_2Mu_2A_2$ 3E (32) $E_5H_3G_3RE_2$ $B_2C_2P_2Mu_2$ 3W (31) $E_5H_3G_3RE_2$ $B_2C_2P_2Mu_2$ A/A_3 HE/HE/Wk/Wk$_2$ Nw/Nw/Mk/Mk$_2$ F/F$_5$ M/M/M$_5$ PEG/PEG/ PEG/PEG$_3$

Figure 1.2 (continued)

HOMEWORK FOR 'THIRD YEAR'	7½ to 9½ hours per week on average.	Board of Education pamphlet on Homework (1937) recommended 1 hour per night for 4 or 5 nights; they found schools gave from 1 to 3 hours per night at this age, with 1½ being usual, for 5 nights.	Much as 1940, that is may vary from 1 to 2½ hours per night; 1½ hours probably average.
DEGREE/TYPE OF DIFFERENTIATION	In practice, there were several possibilities, e.g. 1, 2 or 3 languages, or more Science (perhaps Latin or Physics); for girls Physics or Domestic Science	Spens recommended differentiation for third year as follows: Normal $E.H.G.R1_{10}$ F_4 $M.Sc._7$ $Mu.A.Cr_7PE_4$ $Other_4$ X Course $E.H.G.R1._{10}$ $F.J.*_8M.Sc._6Mu.A.Cr_4PE_4$ $Other_3$ Z Course $E.H.G.R1._{10}F.J.*_{12}$ $M.Sc._6Mu.A.Cr_4PE_4$ $Other_1$ $J* = $ other language(s)	Less differentiation than in '1940' model, because of three year general course. Differences now may only be over second foreign language and sex-linked subjects.
SPECIAL ISSUES	As pupils entered at any age from 10 to 12+, from junior depts., elementary schools or private schools each with differing standards, there might be considerable problems in bringing them up to a comparable level of achievement by the age of about 14. In fact forms were defined by attainment as much as by age. The new girls' schools were modelled on the existing boys' schools, and by 1923* there were many complaints that the curriculum for girls was overloaded and inflexible. Some of the new Municipal Secondary schools had grown out of Higher Grade or Organized Science schools, and set new standards in the teaching of scientific and technical subjects. * when the Report on the Differentiation of the Curriculum was issued.	Much concern with overloading of timetable, for all pupils, and 'academic' nature of curriculum, particuly for the majority who left at 16+. Spens and Norwood reports both advocated lightening the load, by pupils taking fewer subjects from third year onwards. Norwood suggested replacing 'group' exam (School Cert.) by individual subject exam (GCE type) with ultimately, school assessment.	Interest in curriculum planning now focussed on new differentiated pattern for fourth and fifth years; 'options schemes' now beginning to appear, to accommodate growing range of 'academic' subjects, and those practical subjects admitted to GCE range.

Figure 1.3: The 'third year' curriculum in 'non-grammar' schools, 1910–1960

TYPE OF SCHOOL	circa 1910/13 ELEMENTARY	circa 1910/13 HIGHER ELEMENTARY	circa 1940 SENIOR CLASS OR SCHOOL, CENTRAL SCHOOL	circa 1960 SECONDARY MODERN SCHOOL
CONTENT OF 'THIRD YEAR' COURSE	Since pupils could obtain 'full-time exception' at 13 (i.e. could leave school) only a minority would still be at school, mastering 'the elements'.	The middle of a 3 year course (11/12–15); parents often had to promise attendance to 15. (N.B. Not many of these schools were founded, perhaps because of their restricted aims, as defined by regulations)	13–14 pupils might be in an all 'age' school, (discouraged after Hadow (1926) but still present), a senior department or a separate senior school. By 1938 48% of pupils in reorganized schools. Might be selective with a 4 year course (Selective Central) or more commonly non-selective with a 3 year course. (School leaving age raised to 14 in 1922.)	With the school leaving age at 15, third year pupils would either be in penultimate year of 'general' course (or possibly first of two year 'special' course); or would be planning to complete five year course. (approx. 9%)
BACKGROUND OF TEACHERS	About 62% of elementary teachers were 'certificated'; of these 71% of men and 46% of women (who formed two-thirds of the total) were fully trained.	Probably more were college trained. N.B. From 1906, all intending teachers had to have full time secondary education before training.	80% were certificated, and these were mostly college-trained. (2 year course following secondary education), with some specialists in larger schools and a few (7%) graduates. (Training reorganized under Joint Boards after 1925, but distinction remained between 'elementary trained' and 'secondary trained'.)	Some teachers (17%) would be graduates (with or without training) but most would be college trained (2 or 3 years)
EXAMINATION FOR 'THIRD YEAR' PUPILS	None	None. 'Pupils from such schools should not be allowed to prepare for external examinations (Consultative Cttee., 1906)	A few would be aiming for public examinations which had been endorsed by the Hadow Committee who had noted the 'economic value' of such 'tangible evidence of their attainments'. Exams provided by: university bodies, (Matriculation, School Certificate), RSA, College of Preceptors, local bodies (e.g. East Midlands Educ. Union). These usually only in Selective Central Schools; other 'vocational' exams taken by 5–10% of pupils, e.g. Dockyard or Post Office entry.	*Fifth Year* Over 20,000 candidates from Sec. Modern schools entered for GCE O-level in 1959. Still many other exams for fifth year, e.g. RSA, Coll. of Preceptors, Northern Universities' Technical Exam. Council, as well as 'vocational' exams, e.g. Pitman, Army apprentices. *Fourth year* A number of LEAs had instituted 'Leaving Certificate' exams for the upper 30–50% of the ability range. (Only just over half the schools in the 'Newsom' survey entered pupils for these exams.)
TYPE OF TEACHING GROUP	Form group in 'Standard'. 13–14 pupils probably in Standard VII.		Form, often with most 'classroom subjects' taken by form teacher. Streaming common in larger schools – A, B, C streams.	Form: probably streamed, at least to isolate a 'GCE' group and a remedial group; other forms might be parallel. Some specialist teaching. A different-pattern where 'special courses' start in third year (see p. 39)

CONTENT AND STRUCTURE OF 'THIRD YEAR' CURRICULUM	English, Maths, Elem. Science, History, Geography, Cookery/ Laundrywork (girls) Manual Instruction (boys)	English (Lang. & Literature) Elem. Maths, History, Geography, Drawing & manual work (boys), Domestic subjects (girls).	Curriculum for (imaginary) senior *boys'* school 1942 (from Walton, 1972, p. 27)
			
			Third year
			3A (36) M$_6$ E$_6$ Civ$_3$ RI$_1$ Mu$_2$
			       Sc$_3$ PE.G$_4$A$_3$ Wk$_4$MwK$_3$
			
			3B (35) M$_6$ E$_6$ Civ$_3$ RI$_1$ Mu$_2$
			       Sc$_3$ PE.G$_4$A$_3$Wk$_4$MwK$_3$
			
			3C (20) M$_6$ E$_6$ G subjects & REM$_{10}$
			       PE.G$_4$A$_3$Wk$_3$MwK$_3$
			
			   [ ] subjects not taken by form teacher
				Loukes (1956) speaks of a 'long list of subjects' being 'a notable feature of modern schools'. But an integrated approach was also common, based on 'topic work', perhaps under the heading of Social Studies. Timetable outlines under conventional headings may not reveal this, although they will show differences between streams.
				
				3A (30) E M H G RI Mu GSc A Wk/Wk/ PE/PE/PE/
				           Wk/Nw/Mk/DSc·Fr } P/G/G/G/
				3B (36) E M SSt RI Nw/Nw
				3C (37) E M SSt RI Mu GSc A } Mk/Mk/
				           Mu GSc A DSc/DSc
				3D (24) Form teacher RSc·A Wk/Nw Mk/DSc

Figure 1.3 (continued)

HOMEWORK FOR 'THIRD YEAR'	None laid down. Possibly given to older/abler pupils.	Homework usually set only in connection with external exams. In some selective central schools, all pupils might be set homework, about 2 hrs a night for third year pupils, even if only some would enter for exams. (Homework sometimes set in deliberate imitation of grammar schools.) But in non-exam orientated senior schools, little set, often from policy, and some 'leisure' activities provided in lieu. (N.B. Contrast with pre-11+ classes, where scholarship exam pressure resulted in excessive homework. (Board of Education, 1937).		Varied widely, both between schools and between forms. Newsom gave these figures for *fourth* year pupils (1961). Top 25% in ability: 77% in forms with regular homework Middle 50% 52% ,, : : : Lowest 25% (boys) 24% ,, : : : 25% (girls) 36% ,, : : :
DEGREE/TYPE OF DIFFER- ENTIATION	None, except for sex- linked subjects. N.B. In the Central schools opened, e.g. in London and Manchester from 1911, under the Elementary Code, 'biased' commercial/industrial courses were offered to this age group.	Differentiation by streaming had already begun, with the A form studying French and the 'C' form following a 'practical' curriculum; but this was only in the larger, re-organized schools.		Differentiation remained between sex-linked subjects, and might be marked between streams, especially for foreign language. Where special courses began in third year, e.g. commercial, building, engineering, differentiation might be extensive, with group cohering for 'biased' English, Social Studies etc. (N.B. From the Newsom Survey (1961) only 48% of the schools offered subject choice in *fourth* year.)
SPECIAL ISSUES	Although grants for single subjects had been abolished in 1900 in favour of a 'block grant', the curriculum was still narrowly defined in subject terms. Earlier experiments in 'post-primary' vocationally directed education, e.g. the Higher Grade schools and Organised Science schools, had been absorbed into the new secondary school system after 1902. (Grants to higher grade schools were ruled illegal by the Cockerton Judgement.) The Hadow Report (1926) commented: 'Though such experiments have again and again been curtailed or rendered difficult by legislative or administrative action they have persistently re-appeared in various forms. This fact in itself seems to indicate the half-conscious striving of a highly industrialized society to evolve a type of school analogous to and yet distinct from the secondary school, and providing an education designed to fit boys and girls to enter the various branches of industry, commerce and agriculture at the age of 15.' (Hadow Report, p. 34).	The curriculum 'should consist of a few subjects taught as well and sufficiently as possible, rather than a larger number taught superficially'. (1906 instructions.)	'Hadow reorganization' had proceeded at an uneven pace in different LEAs, and was held up by recurrent economic freezes during the 20s and 30s (see p. 37) Levels for selection to grammar school also varied widely—from below 10% to over 30%. The demand for raising the leaving age to 15, which came from many quarters from 1934 on, was not met, despite a fall in numbers on secondary rolls and widespread teacher unemployment.	Some Secondary Modern headteachers strongly disapproved of entering their pupils for public examination, because of the restricting effect this would have on the curriculum of the majority. The Norwood Report (1943) had asked for a common curriculum for all types of school for the first *two* years to facilitate 13+ transfer, but in most areas this was not an important issue in practice. The small number of established comprehensive schools at this date (e.g. in London and Coventry) mostly offered a *three* year common course for all pupils, although this might not include a foreign language for all, and by the third year there might be a number of differences between the streams that were common at this time.

1938) and more carefully developed curricula. Grammar school pupils followed a well-trodden path to school certificate, although as many as 40 per cent of those leaving grammar schools in 1938 had not taken school certificate, and 25 per cent of the pupils had withdrawn before the approved age of sixteen. This was perhaps one indication that all was not well with the grammar school curriculum, a point taken up by the Spens Committee which criticized the course as being too academic, and placing too heavy a burden of work on the average pupil there.[14] 1940, then, represents the 'old' system on the eve of the major changes heralded by the White Paper on Educational Reconstruction (1943) and the 1944 Education Act (the Butler Act). But these changes were concerned primarily with reorganization of the school system and had little immediate effect on the curriculum of any type of secondary school. By 1960, however, a number of factors, some representing official policy, some resulting from pressure and even unilateral action by teachers, had brought marked changes to the secondary school curriculum as a whole, and these were reflected in the circumstances of third year pupils, particularly in secondary modern schools. But, of course, taking a series of cross-sections in this way gives too static a picture; for example, by 1960 experiments were already afoot in some of the new comprehensive schools to develop a common course (that is, common opportunities for all pupils) up to and including the third year, combined with mixed ability teaching and, in some cases, a new radicalism with regard to subject boundaries. The question of what constitutes a 'common course' is discussed in Part III. But for most schools the importance of these innovations lay in the future, and in 1960 the outlines of the third year curriculum in the two main forms of secondary school were sufficiently clear to justify some simple description; it is a reasonable moment at which to take stock.

A. The 13—14 curriculum: the 'grammar school' tradition

If a clear line of descent can be traced for the 1960 grammar school curriculum as a whole from the Regulations of 1904, circumstances had changed considerably by 1960 for pupils in the fulcrum position: the third year of a five-year (main school) course. Most important, this was now seen as the last year of a general foundation course, rather than the first year of course differentiation. This latter scheme had been put forward by the Spens Report as a way of lightening the load created by 'the endeavour to teach a wide range of subjects to the same high level to all pupils'.[15] But the introduction of the GCE examination in 1951 made another solution for the over-crowded timetable possible: now there could be more flexibility about which subjects should be taken and when. At the same time, 'setting', which had been introduced in many schools as a more flexible alternative to streaming, was now seen to have timetabling possibilities for coping with the pressure of new subjects that were becoming accepted into the grammar school timetable, like Russian, technical drawing for boys or commerce for girls. These two pressures resulted in a new look for the fourth and fifth year curriculum, with the beginning of 'option' blocks; the third year curriculum remained in a more 'primitive' form, from a timetabling point of view, with the only differentiation (apart from sex-linked subjects) being in the language area: some pupils would be allowed to take two, or even three, foreign languages. If three were taken, one would probably be Latin. Despite any innovations to be found in particular schools, there had been no radical break with the 'traditional academic curriculum orientated towards the universities', which had been criticized in the Spens Report.[16] The Norwood Report of 1943, in many ways a far more conservative document than its predecessor the Spens Report,[17] considered this tradition in itself would guide the grammar school in its planning:

> 'In the first place we would refer back to an earlier chapter in which we spoke of the essential characteristics of the Grammar School and its purposes for the type of pupil for whom it exists. In setting up its ideal of sound learning, in introducing its pupils to the main departments of human knowledge and experience, in acquainting them with achievements and aspirations of human thought and practice, in training them in the methods and disciplines used by Mathematics, Art, Language, Literature and Natural Science, the Grammar School, if it is to be true to its traditions and its aims, will find a principle by which to test its own curricula. In the second place, the general needs of the pupil who finds his right place in the Grammar School will, on the whole, be much the same, and, though the curricula in this or that Grammar School may vary, they will stand as species to a genus which determines itself through its own intrinsic nature. Thirdly, conferences and exchange of ideas among teachers can do much to create a consensus of opinion unfavourable to ill-judged curricula. Finally, we rely on the sanity and conscience of Head Masters and Head Mistresses.'[18]

Little consideration here for those potential early leavers who might consider this a somewhat stodgy diet. Perhaps they really belonged to that 'type' of pupil destined, in Norwood terms, for the great limbo of the 'modern' school?

B. *The 13—14 curriculum: the 'modern school' tradition*

It is impossible to look back over the history of 'non-selective' or, in pre-1944 terms, 'elementary' education without a deep sense of frustration at the waste of human talent, as well as admiration for those teachers who struggled to offer worthwhile educational experience in very difficult circumstances.[19] The combination of a basically negative official philosophy in the inter-war period[20] and wholly inadequate resources meant that, for the 80 per cent of children not selected for grammar school, the goal set by R.H. Tawney in 1922, *Secondary Education for All*[21] would have a hollow ring to it even after it became official policy in 1944. Of course, it was only after 1947 that all pupils were obliged to complete a third year, with the long postponed raising of the school-leaving age to fifteen, but our concern is to examine what was offered to pupils who remained in school till at least fourteen, and the context in which this education took place.

Even against this background, the *circumstances* of these pupils had changed considerably. In 1910, with the elementary schools confined to their 'post-Morant' role of offering only a limited general education, pupils over thirteen who were still at school would probably be plodding through the traditional curriculum for Standard VII, the 'top class' of the same school which they had attended since they were five, with perhaps some 'enrichment' in the form of practical classes if the facilities were available. By 1940, especially if one went to one of the larger towns, it might indeed seem as if a revolution had taken place. The pupils might be housed in a newly built senior school or at least in a separate senior department. They might have a majority of college trained teachers who were making the most of their 'freedom' from the constraint of public examinations to develop a curriculum which, in this final third year, was allowing for some 'bias' towards vocational courses for which pupils would have been well prepared by their earlier studies of the local area and its development. If the school was large enough, the pupils would probably have been divided on entry into A, B and C streams on the basis of their 'transfer' results, that is, their performance in the 11+ scholarship examination. In fact they might well have been in similar streams throughout their junior schools, since, with the blessing of the psychologists, testing began at an early age. But these pupils would mostly be denied the seal of public examination success, unless in this school the consequence of being in the A stream was an undertaking on the part of the pupil to follow a four or five-year course geared to some form of examination — perhaps even the coveted School Certificate. In some rural areas, however, there might appear to have been few changes since 1910, least of all in the buildings themselves, and it must be remembered that 52 per cent of all 'post-primary' pupils were still in all-age schools in 1938.

This great variation in provision for the age group is a reflection of several factors. First, official policy in the inter-war years in the shape of Education Acts and Board of Education circulars had swung between forward-looking moves like the 1918 Education Act (the Fisher Act), which had raised the school leaving age to fourteen and recommended 'continuation schools' on a part-time basis for those over fourteen;[22] and half-measures like the abortive 1936 Act, which failed to raise the school leaving age to fifteen, allowing only for a system of partial exemptions over fourteen. (This in itself was not to come into force until 1939, and was then postponed indefinitely with the outbreak of war.) There was the same contrast between official Board directives and the recommendations of the Consultative Committee of the Board of Education, which was under the chairmanship of Sir Henry Hadow for most of this period. Thus while later Conservative governments could claim to be carrying out 'Hadow reorganization', in practice the basic recommendations of the Hadow Report, *The Education of the Adolescent* (for secondary education for all, with a leaving age of fifteen), were ignored. In general, official policy seemed to be one of 'no change': education could be accommodated to the social and economic status quo. Intelligence testing, which had become an indispensable part of the educational system in the thirties,* fitted in well in this context. Seen by its advocates — which now included the Board of Education — as a means of achieving a more objective and equitable assessment of pupils' potential, the norm-referenced test approach could be adapted to the particular requirements of selective secondary education, as they were seen at the time. Intelligence testing was not in itself going to prove a case for more secondary school places, and there was a danger that if the new ideas about mental ability were too rigidly interpreted it might seem that large sectors of the population were almost predestined for educational failure. At the same time, the low priority that public elementary education had in government thinking was emphasized by the cuts and freezes that were imposed whenever economic circumstances worsened.

Secondly, and partly as a result of this lack of encouragement from the centre, local authorities responded with differing degrees of enthusiasm to the task of 'Hadow reorganization'.[23] By 1938, Northampton, for example, had reorganized all its elementary schools and could now pay more attention to questions of facilities and curriculum. Indeed, some authorities had made use of the opportunity to raise the leaving age to fifteen by bye-law, enabling teachers to plan a four year course for most pupils. Thirdly, the lack of a clear goal even for the reorganized senior schools meant that there was no real pressure

---

* A Board of Education pamphlet in 1928 described intelligence tests as 'a valuable addition to the armoury of weapons' available for purposes of selection. (Board of Education Pamphlet 63, *Free Place Examinations*, p. 55).

on the less enterprising schools to develop the new curricular outlook
encouraged by the Hadow Report. Indeed, the freedom to experiment
which was enshrined in that Report created problems; as Loukes (1956)
commented:

> 'They [i.e. the members of the Committee] had to describe a new
> type of school, but could not describe it too clearly or they
> would prevent its being what they wanted it to be.'[24]

So although the Committee themselves might be clear about what
should be done to provide a 'modern school curriculum which comes to
a stage of completeness before the children leave'[25], their desire not to
prescribe too closely, particularly as they wished the curriculum to be
related to the local situation, deprived their recommendations of
driving power for all but the more enterprising. In fact, some of their
advice did slowly become part of the conventional wisdom of
secondary modern schools; for example that subjects should be seen as
large units ('English' in place of literature, composition and grammar,
'Mathematics' instead of arithmetic, algebra and geometry), that for
these older pupils there should be 'less formal instruction and more
individual study and written work',[26] and that 'sound teaching must be
based upon the pupil's interests'.[27] But in making these recommendations the Committee acknowledged that they only wished to extend
existing 'good practice' rather than to break new ground. Rather more
effective, judging by subsequent developments, was the advice
contained in Pamphlet 60 issued by the Board of Education in 1928,
under the title *The New Prospect in Education*. Here was the blessing
on a system of A, B and C streams in the senior school, each with its
own curricular level, as, for example, in this arrangement drawn up by
one reorganized school: French only for the A stream, who also took
algebra and geometry, whereas 'an easier course in mathematics is
planned for the B forms, and the C forms take only simple Practical
Arithmetic'.[28]

By 1960, once more the circumstances of these secondary modern
pupils seem to have changed immeasurably, in terms of school
buildings, length of course and access to examinations. Yet the
inequalities of educational provision revealed in the Newsom Report
three years later[29] showed that some of the progress was more apparent
than real. For instance, the Spens Report had recommended a common
course for *all* secondary schools for the first two years, which was to
include one foreign language. But most of the teachers in the secondary
modern schools after the war were still 'elementary trained' and were
not equipped to teach French, so the common course policy was never
implemented, at least in that respect. Where French was taught, it

would in most cases be only for the 'top stream', now being groomed for GCE entry in the fifth year. Again, streaming was still the most likely means of organization, providing at the same time the most obvious form of course differentiation. This might well be formalized into the pattern in Figure 1.2, with a top stream, two middle groups, and a bottom stream following a simple curriculum with a 'modified'[30] scheme of work. In fact, new developments showed up not so much in the framework of subjects presented to third year pupils, as in the possibilities offered by improved facilities, especially for practical subjects; and in the 'topic' or 'project' approach favoured in the classroom.[31] With the leaving age still at fifteen, some headmasters felt it was important to begin 'biased' courses in the third year, although the survey carried out in 1961 for the Newsom Report suggested that even in the fourth year differentiation was only common in the larger schools. A survey published by the Inner London Education Authority in 1967 of work in the first five years of large (comprehensive) school courses gives some interesting information on this. The schools were already geared to a five-year course for most pupils, based on a three-year common course, though often with some sort of streaming. While stressing the desirability of this pattern, the ILEA survey mentions some exceptions:

' . . . While in nearly all the comprehensive schools experience has confirmed the recommendation that for the first three years all pupils should follow a general course which is largely common to all, there is a minority of schools in which the needs of a particular special study give rise to the introduction of a bias into the curriculum of some of the pupils in the third year. Wandsworth and South East London, for example, while keeping the third year course very general, give pupils 'a taste' of building or engineering in the third year. Special arrangements are made at Wandsworth during the third year of any boy's course for him to spend three terms in three different kinds of technical workshop. Catford Boys regroups its pupils for their upper school courses to start in the third year, pupils making their choice of course in the summer term of the second year. At one time in the days when transfer at 13+ was a significant feature of the pattern of secondary education in London, the introduction of specialist courses at the beginning of the third year was much more common that it is now. In two or three schools where headmasters set store by varying the curriculum so that separate sciences are taken and engineering or building courses begun, it is usual to limit the special course work to twenty periods of the timetable. Reasons given are that with earlier maturation, possible leaving at Easter in the fourth year and the need for a course to have relevance, this vocational bias helps to stabilize boys. Most heads, however, believe that deferment of bias until the fourth year is desirable, though the few who introduce it earlier — until the leaving age is raised to sixteen — may rightly urge that they are giving the stimulus stressed in Newsom of 'an education that makes sense'. The inspectors judged, however, that at one such school it would be more beneficial to the pupils if the general course were prolonged for three years.'[32]

Of course, this report, published some time after 1960 and in the context of the comprehensive school, raises issues which were to become increasingly important, in particular the question of a common course for all pupils, in one school, up to and including the third year. I shall return to this issue.

Meanwhile some other points from the Newsom survey are of interest, though the focus there was on the *fourth* year timetable in secondary modern and comprehensive schools. Although the survey showed that there were wide variations among schools in the amount of time given to the three fields of science and mathematics, practical subjects and humanities, the authors found that it was possible 'to identify a typical modern school programme which would be common to most pupils in most schools'.[33] This is reproduced in Figure 1.4. This broad picture shows that a foreign language, while it was a 'serious contender' for inclusion in the modern school curriculum, could not be included in the main diagram since it was taught only to 25—30 per cent of pupils in one-third of the schools in the sample.* It also indicates that the longstanding exhortations to modern schools to provide a 'practical' curriculum had had some effect; practical subjects as defined on the diagram took up 37 per cent of the time in the boys' curriculum, 39 per cent of the girls'. From other evidence it seems likely that the proportion might be rather lower in the third year in most schools. More detailed analysis of the data in relation to subjects revealed some of the marked variations which would not show up in this composite picture. Two main types of variation are discussed. First there is the difference between the time allocation in the 'best fourth year form in a school (A) with that in the poorest fourth year form (C)', and this proved to be important for science, where the A forms in some schools were getting substantially more time than the C forms ('a normal grammar school allowance of time') because they were preparing for external examinations. On the other hand, for

---

*   A larger proportion of pupils may well have learned a foreign language for one or more years, but abandoned it before the fourth year.

Figure 1.4: Fourth year curriculum in a typical secondary modern school

(Reproduced from *Half our Future* (The Newsom Report), 1963, p. 237, by permission of the Controller of HMSO)

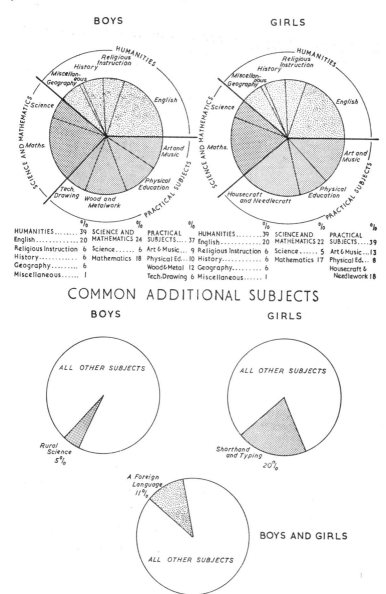

HUMANITIES........ 39   SCIENCE AND   PRACTICAL
English............. 20   MATHEMATICS 24   SUBJECTS.... 37
Religious Instruction 6   Science...... 6   Art & Music... 9
History............. 6   Mathematics 18   Physical Ed... 10
Geography......... 6   Wood&Metal 12
Miscellaneous...... 1   Tech.Drawing 6

HUMANITIES........39   SCIENCE AND   PRACTICAL
English............. 20   MATHEMATICS 22   SUBJECTS.... 39
Religious Instruction 6   Science...... 5   Art & Music...13
History............. 6   Mathematics 17   Physical Ed... 8
Geography......... 6   Housecraft &
Miscellaneous...... 1   Needlework 18

COMMON ADDITIONAL SUBJECTS

mathematics and several practical subjects the main difference in time allocation was between boys and girls, boys having on average more mathematics than girls, but girls being given a greater proportion of time for craft subjects than boys.[34] Some of these distinctions may have appeared only in the fourth year, but it seems likely that some would be relevant to the third year as well. This suggests that although in 1960 the secondary modern schools provided a common *form* of schooling for the majority of the age group, within and between those schools there might be as much variation in curricular provision as there had ever been.

3. The 13—14 Curriculum 1900—1977: general issues

In looking at the changes in the context of the curriculum over the years there have been certain issues which seem to be hardy perennials, coming in for lengthy discussion in every official report, and in other forms of public debate, and decisions on these issues have usually had important consequences for the schools themselves. One of these issues is the relation of public examinations to the curriculum. It has become clear that for the 13—14 age group, differences in curriculum have for much of the century been decided by whether pupils were or were not expected to take a public examination at the end of their 'main school' career, whether they left at fifteen or sixteen. These differences were institutionalized in types of school or, later, in streams within schools. How is it that public examinations acquired this importance, and what functions were they seen as performing? Public examinations, of course, went back to the middle of the previous century, the Education Department themselves being the innovators.[35] By the beginning of this century a wide range of bodies were ooffering their services to schools as examiners and these were welcomed or indeed set up, particularly where there was a pressing need for recognition or accreditation of the course itself.[36] But after 1904 these school courses and their respective examinations were embraced by the *Regulations for Secondary Schools* and a new equation was born: secondary education = examination course, and this had its negative form; *not* secondary education = *not* examination course. This was spelled out in its clearest form in the advice given by the Consultative Committee on the curriculum of the new Higher Elementary school, in 1906:

'Pupils in such schools should not be allowed to prepare for external examinations, as the taking of such examinations was apt to influence unduly the character of the curriculum and to act in the direction of producing a pseudo-secondary school. Further it tended to encourage a deviation from the true type which had been so inimical to the higher grade school.'[37]

This was the first articulation of an official doctrine which was to hold sway until the introduction of the CSE examination in 1964. There seem to be two possible lines of argument behind it. On the one hand, the secondary or grammar school curriculum was seen as 'too narrow' or 'too academic' for most pupils, and teachers outside these schools were urged to seize the opportunity offered by their freedom from examination to experiment and adapt their teaching to the needs of their pupils. This point of view is well put in a Ministry of Education pamphlet in 1945:

'Free from the pressure of any external examination, these schools can work out the best and liveliest forms of secondary education for their pupils. It is essential that they should retain this invaluable freedom which the best of their predecessors used to such advantage, and should be enabled to advance along lines they themselves feel to be right.'[38]

On the other hand, this could be seen as a back-handed way of preserving the privileged position of the grammar schools as the only institutions in the public education system to provide pupils with valid accreditation. The Hadow Report certainly considered that such accreditation should be *available* to all adolescent pupils, even if entry should remain voluntary:

'Boys and girls are handicapped both from the economic and educational standpoints, unless they can produce some tangible evidence of their attainments.'[39]

This point of view would probably have found favour with many parents and teachers and may help to explain the growth of the 'examination industry' in secondary modern schools in the fifties. Indeed, it would be tempting to find a single answer, in the shape of pressure· from such 'clients' of the system as pupils, parents and employers, for the expansion of external examinations since the war and their extension to a much larger proportion of the school population, but obviously there are other important factors, including the fact that examinations are now provided for subjects which in earlier days would have been thought quite unexaminable.[40]

The result of these developments is that public examinations are now provided for an intended 60 per cent of the ability range at 16+;*

---

* In 1974–5, 80 per cent of all pupils leaving school had attained at least one pass in a public examination, (Report of North of England Education Conference, *Times Educational Supplement*, 14.1.77).

surely, then, it could be argued, the distinction between examination and non-examination courses should no longer be regarded as a factor determining or influencing the *third* year curriculum, even if this was the case in the past? This is a question that will be borne in mind in examining the timetables of the schools in the 13—14 Study. In fact it seems that the argument has now shifted from the question of *who* should take examinations (still a live issue in the Newsom Report)[41] to wider issues about the purpose of such examinations for the age group as a whole. The idea of a school-devised leaving certificate as a supplement or even an alternative to a public examination record has come up in some form in almost every report on secondary age pupils written in this century. More recently, it is to be found in the Schools Council report for the 13—16 age group, *The Whole Curriculum*.[42] These broader discussions on the nature and purpose of assessment in school, both internal and external, are likely to be reflected in curriculum planning sessions in the school itself, and since we have already noted the interrelationship between assessment and forms of pupil grouping,[43] it seems likely that attitudes to assessment in general may well have their effect on the way pupils are grouped *throughout* the secondary school, not just in the last two years.

Another recurrent theme which may have some bearing on the third year curriculum can be discussed here briefly. What are the implications of the word 'secondary' for the type of education provided for adolescent pupils? It is now fairly clear that up to 1944 the word was used qualitatively, to denote one particular form of curriculum in a well-established setting, to be distinguished from the other main form, 'elementary'. Any maintained school could be clearly placed by ascertaining whether it came under the 'elementary' or 'secondary' Code of Regulations. But with 'Hadow reorganization' these distinctions had already become unhelpful, and it was not too difficult to gain acceptance for the alternative definition of 'secondary education' which had been outlined by the Hadow Committee in 1926. The essence of this definition is that 'secondary' should denote a *stage* of education, applicable to all pupils and following the primary stage, with the break at eleven or twelve. (This age was accepted as satisfactory on theoretical and practical grounds). It was perhaps inevitable that this watershed should have been over emphasized in the effort to kill off the old 'elementary' image. But by the time of the Newsom Report, another perspective can be seen. According to this, the 'rough administrative division' at eleven between primary and secondary is less than satisfactory on educational grounds:

'This is as straight a frontier in time as the 49th parallel is in space. The trouble is that psychologically eleven is no longer the

watershed it was once thought to be. Different people cross from
childhood into adult life, or rather into the debatable No Man's
Land of adolescence, at considerably different ages. Moreover
many linger behind in childhood in some aspect of life long after
becoming adult in other ways . . . In terms of age the most that
we can safely say is that the frontier of childhood is crossed
during secondary school life . . . '[44]

The authors then go on to give a definition of 'secondary ways of
learning':

> 'The work in a secondary school becomes secondary in character
> whenever it is concerned, first, with self-conscious thought and
> judgment; secondly, with the relation of school and the work
> done there to the world outside of which the pupils form a part
> and of which they are increasingly aware; and, thirdly, with the
> relation of what is done in school to the future of the
> pupils . . . . The transition from primary to secondary in most
> aspects of school work needs to be completed early in the period
> of three years from thirteen to sixteen.'[45]

According to this definition, then, third year pupils are almost
certain to be in a state of transition towards an education which is truly
secondary in character. Is this a widely accepted view, and how would
it be reflected in curriculum planning and organization? It fits with
administrative arrangements like an eleven to thirteen 'lower school' or
a middle school/high school system. But in an 11–18 school the third
year curriculum is usually seen as having more in common with the first
two years than the complex options-based system of the fourth and
fifth years. This is particularly the case where the aim of the school has
been to devise a 'common curriculum' for all pupils in the lower years
of the school. This important development has been closely associated
with pioneering comprehensive schools since 1960, and even before in
some cases. What does it mean in practice, and what are the
consequences for third year pupils?

In 1967, in the ILEA survey of work in their comprehensive schools,
it was claimed that:

> 'The subjects studied in the first three years at a comprehensive
> school are no different from those studied in other schools. All
> pupils in these schools follow for the first three years a general
> course of secondary education which covers the expected range
> of school subjects . . . . Such variety as there is in the choice of
> subjects arises in relation to the study of a foreign language.'[46]

But how much apart from the subject labels is 'common' in this arrangement? The report discusses a number of issues concerning both content and grouping. A common syllabus is seen as highly desirable, but it is pointed out that; 'As a matter of common sense all teachers accept that the pupils in a school catering for a wide range of ability must be taught at different levels.'[47]

The assumption is that in most schools pupils will be 'graded' in terms of ability, although experiments with unstreamed teaching groups in two schools are described. By way of illustration, a geography syllabus is quoted which contains a common core of essential material and various grades of optional topics to be covered by different forms as expedient. This gives a basis for the definition of a common course used by Benn and Simon (1972) in their survey of comprehensive schools, carried out in 1968: 'All pupils pursuing the same basic subjects, even if at a different pace or depth.'[48] Of the 606 11/12+ comprehensive schools in Benn and Simon's survey answering this question, 48 per cent (235) maintained a common course up to fourteen. But even at this general level, perceptions of what constitutes a common course may differ: only 42 per cent of those schools which claimed to provide a common course offered a foreign language to *all* their pupils in the year in which a foreign language was begun in the school. It almost seems as if a common course is now seen as the one desirable goal which, like virtue, all must be seen to be pursuing, whatever the context and circumstances of the school. But how can one compare the common course of a three form entry grammar school with that devised for a comprehensive high school with a year group of 350 taught in mixed ability classes? So there are numerous problems of definition in the idea of a common course for the third, or any other, year; and even if it is *possible* to offer such a course (and many schools may consider it is not), it does not follow that all will consider it desirable. Certainly, issues like these will be central to our own inquiry into the framework for the third year curriculum. It will also be important to look at developments that have sometimes followed in the wake of the common course: for instance, integration across subject boundaries and experiments in team teaching. The ILEA survey talks of such developments moving in to the lower years of the secondary school possibly as a result of integration of learning in the primary school; but this raises the question of how often such experiments are laid aside before the third year.

It should be emphasized that many of these developments have taken place in comprehensive schools which, although they tended at first to be 'quite conservative' nevertheless 'created an environment which was more conducive to change than that of the grammar or secondary modern school.'[49] Some teachers came to the early comprehensive schools, for example, because they were dissatisfied with such practices as streaming and 'many of these teachers were pressing for internal reorganization within the schools during the first honeymoon period of reorganization.'[50] The other obvious feature of these early comprehensive schools is that they were usually large — 1500 pupils or more. Even if the organizational problem was to be tackled on conventional lines, with differentiation (or streaming) by ability throughout the school, the sheer size of the task might be daunting. The call for new types of grouping, new subjects, more choice for more pupils, and new ways of distributing staff resources meant that the old ways of creating the school timetable were seen to be inadequate even as highly skilled staff struggled to piece together the 'very complicated and perhaps quite impossible jigsaw'.[51] But, as the politicians are always telling us, challenges can become opportunities; and the development of the art (or science) of timetabling in recent years has in itself created new possibilities for the organization of the curriculum in all types of school by developing a new language in which to discuss the problems and explore possible solutions.

These new developments in timetabling and school organization are most closely associated with the name of Davies (1969), who adapted forms of organizational analysis from other fields in order to lay bare the laws governing the school curriculum. Already a new generation of headmasters and directors of curriculum has been initiated at conferences into these mathematically-based model-building techniques. But Davies stressed that it was not his intention to create a new orthodoxy or a set of blueprints; on the contrary, the point of a numerical matrix was to open up a wider field of choice:

'Without some notation of the kind that the matrix supplies, we are less well equipped to explore the possibilities of curriculum pattern than we are to accept the stereotyped interpretation of it which practice and custom have bequeathed to us as legacies from the educational past.'[52]

In a foreword to Walton's collection of timetable studies, Davies traces the downgrading of the 'form' as the main timetabling unit and the successive appearance of setting, mixed ability tutor groups, banding, and faculty structure as a series of expedients each brought in to 'cancel out the ill effects, or unfortunate side effects of the last invention'.[53] Davies considers this to be an inefficient way of 'lurching forward', and favours instead a systems analysis approach by which experts could set out all the models which could be derived from the finite grid of a school timetable. This would then free head teachers and other educational planners to develop their plans and schedules with all the models to choose from. At present, however, it would probably be more realistic to think of these planners using the new techniques to lay bare the structure of their own familiar model in order to improve its efficiency or perhaps to compare it with other (similar) models in use elsewhere. But even this limited use would bring familiarity with concepts like the bonus class, transverse matrix and the primary group, which would soon make the task of curriculum planning and the consequent timetabling take on quite a new look.

Once more it is relevant to ask: 'What about the third year?' Is this approach likely to have any particular consequences for them? According to Davies' own description, his analysis only serves to bring out more clearly the latent assumptions about the place of the third year in the school as a whole. For example, he shows how it is possible by some fairly simple calculations to work out the 'bonus pattern' for a school, that is the amount of spare teaching capacity for a given number of pupils and teachers. This will show the head teacher how many 'bonus classes', or units of spare capacity, he has to distribute among the year groups in the school, after a common basic allocation has first been made to each year group according to the number of pupils involved. The effect:

> 'is to sharpen the headmaster's view of his job in drafting a curriculum by presenting it to him as a matter only of distributing the . . . bonus classes.'[54]

How should this distribution be made? From a technical point of view the answer is arbitrary, so the head teacher will go back to the customary practice of the school for guidance. Davies explains how a formula could be developed:

> 'Pupils in their first two years follow by and large a common curriculum; so that the two year groups concerned have usually the same number of classes organized for them. Again, by and large, the curriculum's options will all have arisen by the start of the fourth school year, so that if attendance is compulsory to the age of sixteen the fourth and fifth year groups will . . . want the same number of classes allocated to them . . . True there is some room for manoeuvre in the case of the third year group, which may either continue with the common curriculum, or begin the fully differentiated course, or else occupy an intermediate position that entails a limited amount of differentiation of studies. But we have only to determine the status of this third year group, in the light of the average practice of schools, and immediately, since the rest of the structure is rigid, it becomes

possible for us to define, in *relative terms*, the components of a model to replicate the curriculum of a main school with a known number of bonus classes.

    . . . On the evidence available, the average practice is to fix the third-year bonus at about a third of the way between the second and fourth year bonus figures (i.e. if the second and fourth year groups have two and eight bonus classes respectively, then the third year group is likely to have a four class bonus).'[55]

This is to give mathematical precision to that intermediate, halfway position which we have suggested is often carved out for the third year. But it is only fair to point out that this is merely one application of a method which could be adapted to distribute the 'bonus' quite differently, — for example in order to make special provision for backward pupils in the first three years. So a new approach to timetabling could in fact be one way of enabling the planner to look more carefully at the position of third year pupils who may be sandwiched rather uneasily between the 'lower school' and the fourth year options system, and to perceive the possibilities for them, not only in terms of subjects to be offered but also in the allocation of time and the forms of grouping.

    Today, 13-14-year-old pupils may find themselves in a school where the questions of what they should learn, and in what context, have been the subject of radical discussion and planning, all from the standpoint of present day needs and concerns; but it is more likely that the schools and those who teach in them have been shaped and influenced in varying degrees by what has been done in the past. And once one looks into the past one can see a number of strands that have become wound — or tangled — together to form new patterns. According to Davies, the school timetable in itself:

'although a rich mine of information, has little but toil and sweat to offer to someone who wants to extract the precious ore from it'[56]

but by looking at timetables and other relevant data from one hundred Midlands schools we hope it will be possible to discover the patterns of curriculum organization that third year pupils are likely to encounter today, and the contexts in which these patterns may be found.

Notes

1. Walton, J., (Ed). *The Secondary School Timetable*, Ward Lock Educational, 1972, pp. 18, 29.

2. Davies, T.I., *School Organisation*, Pergamon Press, 1969, p. 58.

3. By the Prefatory Memorandum to the Regulations for Secondary Schools approved by Robert Morant, Permanent Secretary of the Board of Education in 1904: 'For the purpose of these Regulations, therefore, the term "Secondary School" will be held to include any Day or Boarding school which offers to each of its scholars, up to and beyond the age of 16, a general education . . . given through a complete graded course of instruction.' As J.S. Maclure points out, these regulations 'effectively ensured that the new County Secondary schools to be established under the powers given to the Local Education Authorities under the Act [1902 Education Act] should follow closely the conventional pattern of the old public and grammar schools.' Maclure J.S., *Educational Documents, England and Wales*, Methuen, p. 156—7.

4. Lewis Report: *Report of the Departmental Committee on Juvenile Education in relation to Employment after the War*, Board of Education, 1917, p. 5—7.

5. Recommendations: *Report of the Consultative Committee of the Board of Education on the Education of the Adolescent*, (The Hadow Report), 1926, p. 70—96.

6. *Report of the Consultative Committee of the Board of Education with special reference to Grammar Schools and Technical High Schools*, (The Spens Report), 1938.

7. *Report of the Committee of the Secondary Schools Examinations Council on Curriculum and Examinations in Secondary Schools*, (The Norwood Report), 1943.

8. Loukes, H., *Secondary Modern*, Harrap, 1956.

9. The importance of this uniformity had been recognized since 1938 when the Spens Report commented: 'Parity among schools . . . implies the raising of the minimum leaving age to the same general levels in these schools.' A leaving age of 16 was not immediately attainable, but . . . must now be envisaged as inevitable'. Spens (1938), p. 311.

10. In seven local education authorities in England and Wales less than 10 per cent of the age group were offered grammar school places (Loukes (1956), p. 37). Loukes remarks that by 1955 some secondary modern pupils were getting up to six GCE O-level passes.

11. *Secondary Education for all, a new drive*, Ministry of Education, HMSO, 1958.

12. Circular 10/65, *The Organisation of Secondary Education*, issued by the Department of Education and Science, 12.7.65. This circular invited LEAs to submit plans for the reorganization of their secondary schools in order to eliminate selection into separate and different types of secondary school at eleven.

13. Benn, C. and Simon, B. *Half Way There*, (second edition) Penguin, 1972, p. 114.

14. Spens Report (1938), p. 71—3.

15. Op. cit., p. xxiii.

16. Op. cit., p. 73.

17. The Norwood Committee was an *ad hoc* subcommittee of the Secondary Schools Examination Council, and was appointed, according to Simon (1974) 'to neutralize the recommendations of the Consultative Committee' — (i.e. the Spens Report). It produced recommendations in line with official Board of Education thinking; in fact, the report 'proved almost more than had been hoped for', with its elaboration of 'types of child mind' numbering

exactly three. Moreover, it was published directly by the President of the Board before it could be considered by the Secondary Schools Examination Council. Those in power 'adopted the Norwood Report as the Tables of the Law.' (Simon, B. *The Politics of Educational Reform, 1920–1940*, Lawrence & Wishart, 1974, pp. 323, 327–8.)

18. Norwood Report (1943), p. 72.
19. 'In the memory of those who lived through them, the inter-war years were dominated by the cry for and practice of economy. In the elementary schools particularly, expenditure was cut to the bone, everything done on the cheap.' Simon, (1974), p. 294.
20. Simon (1974) has argued that the Board of Education throughout this period, often with the tacit agreement of the government of the day, was:

> 'geared from the start to programme secondary education only for an elite with, for the majority, merely ancillary provision to promote togetherness in the tasks of making capitalist industry and social relations work.' (P. 318)

Given the dedication of many of the Board's servants to the improvement of the 'post-primary sector' it might be judicious to attribute the lack of progress to a number of pressures from outside education rather than to any deliberate conspiracy against 'the masses'.

21. Tawney, R.H. *Secondary Education for All : a statement of Labour Policy*, Allen and Unwin, 1922.
22. The failure of the continuation schools in some areas was in part due to parental objections, but the delays in implementing the 1918 Education Act which provided for continuation schools coincided with a fierce government economy drive (from 1921). Circular 1190, issued to local authorities by the Board of Education in January 1921 encouraged only the preparation of plans; no financial assistance could be expected except for the most urgent projects, and continuation school plans already approved were to be shelved. By the end of 1922 those local authorities which went ahead with continuation schools had been obliged to abandon them — with the single exception of Rugby.
23. There were additional legal and administrative problems in instituting changes for any authority with a large proportion of church schools, as, for example, in Manchester and Preston.
24. Loukes (1956), p. 24.
25. Op. cit., p. 48.
26. Hadow (1926), p. 103.
27. Op.-cit., p. 107
28. Board of Education, Pamphlet No. 60, (1928), *The New Prospect in Education*, p. 40. (The arrangement quoted in the text applied to a county borough described in an appendix.)
29 In the survey conducted for the Newsom Committee in 1961, covering a national sample of secondary modern and comprehensive schools, it was found that two-fifths of the schools were in 'seriously inadequate' premises. Only one-quarter had an adequate library room, and one-third had no proper science laboratories. In addition, staff turnover was high, and the Committee found considerable dissatisfaction with 'irrelevant' school work particularly among older pupils. *Half our Future* (HMSO), 1963, pp. 10–11.
30. The word used for the scheme of work followed in the lower stream in junior schools in 1928 Pamphlet No. 60 (Board of Education).
31. The 'topic' approach was strongly advocated in the NUT Report '*The*

Curriculum of the Secondary School' (1952), and detailed suggestions, given in an appendix.

32. Inner London Education Authority, *London Comprehensive Schools, 1966, 1967*, p.60.

33. Newsom Report (1963), p. 236.

34. Op. cit., p. 239—241.

35. 'Perhaps as an act of divine retribution, the profession that was to inflict the examination system on the rest of society was the first to be its victim. The first tests for a teacher's certificate, for instance, were held almost a decade before either the Civil Service Commissioners or the General Medical Council began their work.' Hurt, *Education in Evolution*, Paladin, 1972, p. 129.

36. The Cambridge Higher Local Examination was established as early as 1869 specifically for women and girls originally as a 'tertiary' examination to be taken after they had left school. But it became part of the sixth form course and was used by girls 'as an avenue to the university'. *Report of the Board of Education Consultative Committee on the Differentiation of the Curriculum for Boys and Girls*, HMSO, 1923, p. 31.

37. Quoted in the Hadow Report (1926), p. 30—31.

38. Ministry of Education, Pamphlet No. 1, *The Nation's Schools, their plans and purpose*, 1945, p. 21.

39. Hadow Report (1926), p. 151.

40. Op. cit., p. 157 ff.

41. The Newsom Report, written while the new Certificate of Secondary Education was in the planning stage, accepted reluctantly that 'examinations are here to stay, and as time goes on the tendency is always for more rather than fewer pupils to be involved'. At the same time they wished to 'reiterate the statement of the Crowther Report: "in some subjects a good modern school education seems to us very difficult to reconcile with an external examination . . . . ." '. (Newsom (1963), p. 81).

42. See, particularly, the Norwood Report which recommended a 'school certificate' of a profile type for all pupils coupled with teacher-directed examinations for grammar school pupils. The authors had noted that: 'If the present School Certificate is retained without alteration . . . . a system will . . . . be established under which parity in secondary education will become impossible'. In *The Whole Curriculum 13—16* (Schools Council Working Paper 53, Evans/Methuen Educational, 1975) school based assessment is discussed on pp. 101—115.

43. In particular, the simultaneous growth of 'intelligence testing' for all eleven-year-olds, and streaming within the schools at both Junior and Senior level, during the 1930s.

44. Newsom Report (1963), p. 112.

45. Op. cit., p. 112—113.

46. ILEA (1967), p. 59.

47. Op. cit., p. 60.

48. Benn and Simon (1972), p. 215.

49. Walton (1972), p. 43

50. Op. cit., p. 43.

51. Op. cit., p. 46.

52. Davies (1969), p. 51.

53. Davies, T.I. in Walton (1972), p. 10.

54. Davies (1969), p. 93.

55. Op. cit., p. 121—2.

56. Op. cit., p. 7.

PART II

The Outline and Structure of the Third Year Curriculum: A Survey of 100 Schools, 1974/75

Introductory

Part II is concerned with information derived from the second of three questionnaires sent to participating schools in 1974. This second questionnaire was entitled 'The Third Year Curriculum', and through it an attempt was made to obtain a picture of the general structure of the curriculum in each school as it affected the 'third year', that is pupils aged 13–14. When the questionnaire was being drafted the problem was to find terms which would convey, as far as possible, a common meaning, but which were sufficiently precise for schools to be clear about whether or not the terms applied to them. First impressions suggested that most respondents had felt able to describe the bare bones of their curriculum in answer to our questions. Three schools were visited so that some details could be clarified or amplified, and while such visits, even brief ones, helped considerably in adding depth to the picture, they also established some face validity for the questionnaire by showing that this fuller picture was in keeping with the answers supplied by the respondents.

The data from all the schools will be described in several sections. The first considers the way the third year timetable was structured in the schools. This is followed by an outline description of third year activities in school. In the third section, the ways in which pupils are grouped for work are explored. The final section looks at the less tangible aspects of the third year curriculum; how, in an ideal world, would the curriculum differ from present reality, and what are the constraints which hinder the school from implementing desired changes? An abbreviated version of the questionnaire is attached as Appendix B so that reference can be made to the original questions.

This survey does not include any discussion of the arrangements made for remedial teaching in the third year. Some information was obtained about the amount of remedial provision in the schools; two-thirds of the schools organized some third year remedial teaching, most of them (53) having a special remedial department. The proportion of pupils receiving this help varied widely, from a handful (two per cent) to one-third of the year group. But it was felt that the organization and methods used for remedial teaching could not be adequately studied in this wider survey of the curriculum. Therefore in many of the questions about the organization of third year work respondents were asked not to include any *group* of pupils who constituted a separate remedial class. (See Appendix B for details of these instructions.)

1. Allocation of time

At the beginning of the survey, questions were asked about the overall allocation of time within the school. Were some, or many, schools operating outside the familiar five-day, 40-minute period format? (Q, p. 1, no. 1).* The answer at first sight seems to be 'no' (see Table 2.1 (a)(b)). Eighty-six of the 100 schools had a five-day cycle and 90 divided each day into 'single periods of less than 50 minutes' (Q, p. 1, no. 1c), at least for the third year. Six schools had a ten-day cycle, and there were a few with other patterns, three of which were boarding schools. There was even less variation in the type of time unit used within the third year timetable. Only six schools had single periods of more than 50 minutes, although three had a mixed pattern of longer and shorter periods.

Table 2.1: Allocation of time for the third year

(a)	*Length of timetable cycle*	Number of Schools
	5-day timetable cycle	86
	5½-6 day timetable cycle	7
	8-day timetable cycle	1
	10-day timetable cycle	6
		100

(b)	*Length of single periods*	
	All single periods of less than 50 mins.	90
	All single periods of more than 50 mins.	6
	Some long and some short periods	3
	No response	1
		100

(c)	*Proportion of timetable as double periods*	
	No double periods	2
	Less than 33% of timetable as double periods	34
	33—50% of timetable as double periods	18
	Over 50% of timetable as double periods*	43
	No response	3
		100

*   This includes the six schools with single periods of over 50 minutes.

It is, however, important to see these responses in the light of the next question, on the use of 'double periods' for the third year. Schools were asked what proportion of the third year timetable consisted of

*   All references to items from the Timetable Questionnaire, (Appendix B) will be given in the form: Q (Questionnaire), p.1, (Page number), no.1, (question number).

double periods. The responses are given in Table 2.1(c). Clearly, a considerable number of schools made generous use of double periods; 43 out of the 97 schools responding to this item had 50 per cent or more of the third year timetable in double periods, and only two were making no such provision. It would seem that in some cases the 'single period of less than 50 minutes' is a notional item — 'book-keeping' for the timetable — so that for most of the time pupils' experience would be of blocks of 80 minutes or so. These schools, though nominally working a day of seven or eight 40 minute periods at the third year level, were in practice dealing much of the time in a different sort of currency — a majority of 'long' sessions with a sprinkling of single periods here and there.

This division of time, and the purposes it may serve, can be seen in another way in the responses to the questions about 'blocking'. This is a process whereby, for example, all the pupils in the third year, or a whole band, may have one subject — 'English' — on the timetable at the same time, and probably for an appreciable lenth of time. This gives the teachers concerned the option of planning that time as they see fit. They may all continue to teach their classes as before, but it will be possible to assemble the whole year group together for a film or a lecture, or to re-divide them into as many sub-groups as seem desirable. Schools were asked if their timetable was planned to make use of 'blocking' in this way (Q, p. 10—11, no. 4): 40 out of 99 of the respondents confirmed that this was their intention. Some gave further details; for example, in one school several subject areas were listed here with the following comments:

| History | — | Integrated humanities work, team teaching and field work. |
| Music | — | Regrouping for practical choral and instrumental work. |

In another school the arrangements were described thus:

PE	—	Large group activities and variations in team games.
Practical subjects in lower band	—	Regrouped to make a viable number in each subject.
Science	—	Group lectures occasionally or for talks or for 'circus' experiments under Nuffield scheme.

In this section, several subjects were mentioned very frequently; for example, craft subjects were very often blocked so that regrouping could take place either on a sex basis or to fit in with available staff and rooms. Sometimes the aim was to allow pupils to 'rotate' from one craft area to another. Physical education (PE) was frequently block-timetabled to give staff freedom to arrange varied programmes of activities. Less often there was a clear reference to the type of year group lecture or film mentioned earlier. The clearest example of this comes from a mixed high school.*

English	Key lesson and A/V sessions
Social Studies	followed by group activities.
Science	Use is made of facilities of
Maths	theatre and large lecture room.
Craft	

These glimpses of the real world of the school confirmed that there may be a considerable amount of flexibility concealed within a conventional timetable framework.

Most school timetables lay claim to another portion of time outside the normal school hours: homework time. At this stage only simple qeustions were asked about the proportion of pupils doing homework and the time allocated to it (Q, p. 12, no. 6). The details on homework provision are given in Table 2.2.

Table 2.2: Homework provision for third year pupils

(a)	*Percentage of pupils regularly set homework*	Number of Schools
	All pupils are set homework	67
	65—94% of pupils are set homework	17
	Less than 60% of pupils are set homework	13
	No response	3
		100
(b)	*Average time spent on homework per day*	
	30—45 minutes per day	5
	60 minutes per day	35
	75—90 minutes per day	36
	105—120 minutes per day	16
	No response	8
		100

* This is the school referred to in Part 3 as 'West Mercia High School'. For further details of the third year curriculum there, as it was in 1975—6, see pages 94—104.

It can be seen from this that most third year pupils at all types of schools questioned were expected to do an appreciable amount of homework every night. Sixty-seven out of the 97 schools set homework for all their pupils; only 19 had fewer than 75 per cent of their pupils fully occupied in this way. Again, for most pupils the time allocated to homework would be between 1 and 1½ hours (71 out of 93 schools). Sixteen schools expected more than this; of these, 10 schools assigned 2 hours on average each night for homework. No questions were asked at this stage about the type of work set for homework, or the way in which it was allocated. But clearly this was an area that needed further exploration. Was it possible that with the growth of comprehensive schools the homework industry, formerly thriving chiefly in the grammar school context, had expanded? If so, what function was homework intended to have for most pupils, and in how many schools was a strict homework formula adhered to at the third year level? All that could be said from these data was that homework figured unmistakably in the daily pattern of the majority of 13-14-year-olds. During Stage Two of the study more detailed questions about homework were asked in the eighteen 'background schools' and in the two 'case study' schools, and this resulted in *Homework: a Case for Study* (another publication in this series).

2. Third year activities
A. Curricular patterns

What pattern of curriculum was offered to the third year in the sample schools? Respondents were asked to answer this question by completing a simple type of grid (Q, p. 5, no. 3a) for all pupils aged 11−16, indicating for each age group whether there was a common curriculum, a curriculum where *most* subjects were done by all pupils, or some type of options system. The exact wording of the items is given in Table 2.3. It is difficult to know whether the wording of this sort of item will be interpreted in the same way by all respondents; there are some indications from checks with other data, that not all schools took fully into account the number of minority subjects actually being taught in the third year. For this analysis, only responses describing the pattern of the curriculum for the third year were considered and the overall picture, according to the perceptions of the respondents, is given in Table 2.3.

It seems clear from this table that in most cases nearly all the third year pupils within a school would be following a common course outline for most of the time. The main exceptions would be, firstly, those areas where separate activities were timetabled for boys and for girls − for example Craft and PE; and secondly, the learning of a first or second foreign language by a minority of pupils. It would perhaps be helpful to

Table 2.3: Curricular patterns for third year pupils

		Number of Schools
(i)	Every pupil follows the same activities though pace, balance and content may differ.	12
(ii)	Same as (i) above *except* that boys and girls may follow different activities in some parts of the timetable (e.g. Domestic Science/Handicrafts).	16
(iii)	*All* or *some* pupils follow *one or two* activities not common to all (e.g. an extra language).	62
(iv)	*All* or *some* pupils follow *three or more* activities not common to all.	9
	No response	1
		100

fill out this picture by describing in more detail some schools which appear to typify the different categories.

Common course outline for all third year pupils

School A was a boys' grammar school, offering a common course outline to all its pupils, by definition a sub-group of the local population of 13- to 14-year-olds. They studied the following subjects in basic teaching groups, which were defined for the purposes of the questionnaire as the groups in which pupils spent 50 per cent or more of their timetabled periods:

Subject	Number of periods per timetable cycle
English	4
History	2
Geography	2
French	4
Latin	4
German	3
Maths	5
Biology	2
Chemistry	2
Physics	2
Art	2
Music	2
PE	1

With one or two subjects some juggling of numbers and time had been done in order to fit in with other groups or with the facilities available:

Pottery	(Pottery in sub-groups	2
Woodwork	in rotation)	
Religious Education (RE)		1 } Blocked. Games
Games		2 } grouped vertically
		with fourth and
		fifth years

In School B, another boys' school, there was also a common course outline for all third year pupils, but in the rather different context of a large comprehensive school. In their mixed ability basic teaching groups, pupils studied the following subjects:

Subject	Number of periods per timetable cycle
Mathematics	2
English	2
History	1
Geography	2
RE	1
French	2
PE	1
Games	1
Metalwork	1
Music	1
Art	½
Home Economics	½
Physics	1
Chemistry	1
Biology	1
Geology	1
Technical Drawing	1

It will be noticed that the total number of periods taught was 20; these periods were units of 70 minutes, representing one half of a ten-day timetable cycle, a rather different pattern from the 'norm' described on page 56.

Another type of common course outline to be found in some large comprehensive schools is really a common *framework* allowing for a considerable degree of flexibility for regrouping pupils or subjects. Thus in school C the curriculum consisted of a small number of subject areas, but one of these might embrace several conventional 'subjects'. For example, 'Communications' covered English, English for Immigrants, and French; and whereas all pupils might study *English* in their basic teaching groups only some of the third year would take French, and not all would be in need of specialized English Language teaching.

These distinctions are not intended to imply that one type of common course outline is 'better' than another, but just to give some indication of the different realities existing behind the one label, even within the comparatively crude categorization of a questionnaire.

Common course outline, except for 'sex-linked' subjects

The second category of curricular types applied to mixed schools where some subjects could only be taken by one sex. It should be noted that a few schools (where from the timetable details given later this pattern clearly obtained), apparently did not see themselves as restricting subjects in this way.

Some subjects are problematical in this context; how far is 'Games' a subject open to all when in practice boys play rugger and girls play netball? Perhaps this is unimportant, but in other parts of the curriculum the issue is more debatable. Is it desirable to have all courses open to both sexes and, if desirable, is it feasible within a particular school? The most sensitive area seems to be that covering aesthetic and practical subjects. In this area the need for small groups, and the widespread shortage of craft specialists and suitable rooms and equipment, may be more powerful factors than theoretical consideration of sex bias.

What about some 'typical' schools in this category? In school D, rural science, woodwork and metalwork were restricted to boys, home economics and needlework to girls. Interestingly, technical drawing, another common 'boys only' subject, was taken by all. No comment was made about these divisions. At school E, however, where there was a similar pattern of boys' and girls' crafts, there was concern about the arrangement and on another page of the questionnaire it was stated that future third year pupils would have a free choice of crafts.

It should be pointed out that these curricular differences for boys and girls apply to mixed schools; far greater differences may exist between the curricula of single-sex schools, which would not have shown up in this part of the questionnaire. For example, in a survey of the curriculum by the Department of Education and Science[1] it was shown that over all types of secondary schools there were some marked differences between the sexes for some 'mainstream' subjects studied in the third year. For example, physics was taken by 36 per cent of boys and only 17 per cent of girls, but for biology the position was almost reversed, with 29 per cent of boys and 50 per cent of girls taking it. Rather more girls than boys studied modern languages (52 per cent of girls, 46 per cent of boys), but there was little difference for maths, English, history and geography. The craft subjects were almost exclusively linked to one sex or the other.

Common core curriculum, with one or two 'minority' subjects

The third type of course outline, where most subjects were taken by all third year pupils, but where there were one or two 'minority' subjects (other than remedial provision), was found in 62 of the 100 schools. One or two examples will suffice. School F exemplified this category well. The only subject not common to all pupils, at first sight, was French; only 70 of the 235 third year pupils studied French — that is those in the top two forms of a streamed intake. Closer inspection shows that in practice there was some sex differentiation in Craft and PE, so that there were probably some types of craft which were restricted to a sub-group of pupils in the same way as in schools D and E. Another example coming within this category is of a school where the minority subject was a second foreign language. Thus, in school G, a girls' grammar school, the only subjects not common to all were Latin and German; Latin was taken by 30 of the 90 third year pupils, German by 38. All pupils had begun one or other of these languages in the second year but could give it up in the third year.

A number of schools found in this category seemed to be offering more than two minority subjects even when sex-differentiated subjects were excluded. Thus in school H, the following curricular pattern obtained:

Subject	Number of periods per timetable cycle	
English	5	
Maths	5	
Geography	2	
History	2	Taken by all pupils
Science	6	
Art	2	
PE	3	
Needlework	3	Taken by girls
Home Economics	3	
Combined Craft	6	Taken by boys
French or European Studies	5	
German	4	Guided choice
Rural Science	2	
Music	2	

This curriculum pattern, which appears more complex than some considered so far, immediately raises the question which in fact applies to all curricula in this category: how do some pupils make time for minority subjects? No direct question was asked about this but there are plainly several possibilities. Where there is a straight choice between, for example, French and European Studies, it may simply be a question of regrouping pupils for a block of time. But when the minority subjects are extra to the rest of the curriculum either the pupils must give up another whole subject or spend less time on several subjects. It could sometimes be inferred from the details given in the questionnaire that pupils taking extra subjects did spend less time than the rest of the group on 'mainstream' subjects. It seems likely that the same variety of problems could then arise which afflicts the planning of a complex options-based timetable; problems which may well concern those schools in the next curriculum category to be described.

Common core curriculum with options for most pupils

For nine schools, the third year curriculum seemed to fit best into this last category, that is, where all or some pupils followed three or more activities not common to all. On examination, some of these curricula seemed not to differ markedly from a number placed in the previous category; it was partly a question of how the rubric had been interpreted. Certainly, no school was operating a full scale options system with a range of choices for all pupils. The schools which placed themselves in this category seemed to fall into three groups. For the first group (three schools), the choices were related primarily to languages; for example, pupils studying one or two foreign languages would have less art or craft than other pupils and might miss some activities (for example, outdoor pursuits) completely. In the second group (also three schools), for different bands or streams there were differences in the subjects studied which really amounted to distinct curricula for the various groups. In one of these schools the top band took physics, chemistry and biology, the lower band had more craft choices. In another school the choice seemed more drastic: *either* physics, chemistry and biology, *or* art, needlework and domestic science. Particular problems arise with 'banded curricula' of this type; what of the pupil who is 'promoted' to a higher band, and has never studied French? One school's answer was to provide a separate option, 'business studies', for these pupils. More flexibility can be achieved where there are options within each course as was the case with the third group of schools: one of these provided three courses, each having options within it. This school, and one other offering several options in the third year, both had a selected third year group; this might be a sign of early specialization by able pupils.

B. Subjects on offer in the third year: an overview

In the Timetable Questionnaire, a double-page grid was provided for a bare outline of the schools' third-year curriculum. (Q, p. 6–7, no 3a). From this source a rather simple description could be constructed of the range of subjects on offer to 13-14-year-old pupils. It is clearly recognized that the subject descriptions given in this grid were labels only, and the activities they stood for might vary widely from school to school, and class to class. Moreover, while teachers might think that they would at least have common expectations about the meaning and

Figure 2.1: A summary of third year curriculum descriptions.

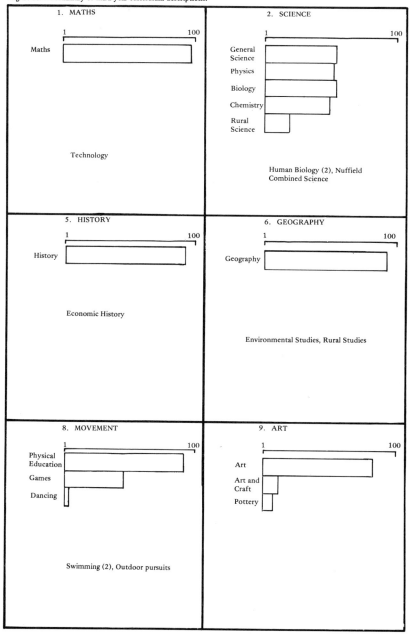

Figure 2.1 cont'd.

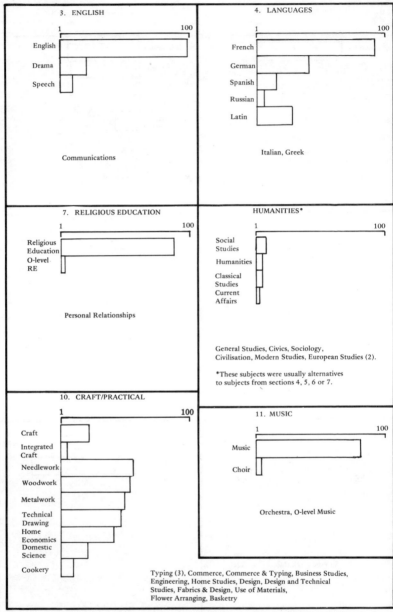

3. ENGLISH

English
Drama
Speech

Communications

4. LANGUAGES

French
German
Spanish
Russian
Latin

Italian, Greek

7. RELIGIOUS EDUCATION

Religious
Education
O-level
RE

Personal Relationships

HUMANITIES*

Social
Studies
Humanities
Classical
Studies
Current
Affairs

General Studies, Civics, Sociology,
Civilisation, Modern Studies, European Studies (2).

*These subjects were usually alternatives
to subjects from sections 4, 5, 6 or 7.

10. CRAFT/PRACTICAL

Craft
Integrated
Craft
Needlework
Woodwork
Metalwork
Technical
Drawing
Home
Economics
Domestic
Science
Cookery

11. MUSIC

Music
Choir

Orchestra, O-level Music

Typing (3), Commerce, Commerce & Typing, Business Studies,
Engineering, Home Studies, Design, Design and Technical
Studies, Fabrics & Design, Use of Materials,
Flower Arranging, Basketry

Note. The scale in each section indicates the number of schools offering the subject. Subjects listed at the foot of each section were mentioned once only, unless otherwise indicated.

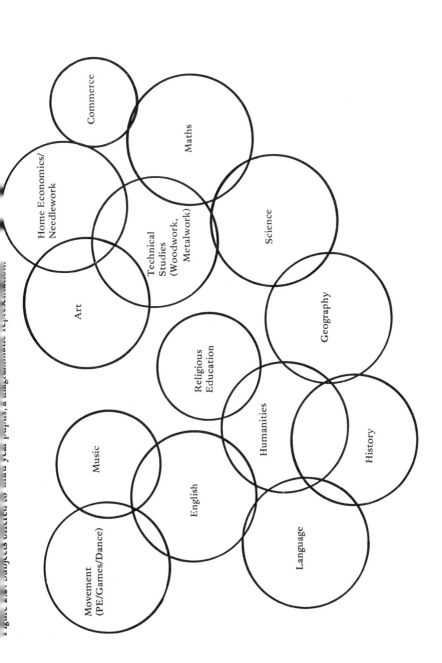

Figure 2.1 Subjects offered to third-year pupils, a diagrammatic representation.

content of, say, maths at the third year level, it would be very difficult to come to any generally acceptable definition of 'humanities'; and a label like 'craft' may refer to some widely differing groups of activities.

With these reservations in mind, two types of data summary were constructed (see Figures 2.1 and 2.2). Figure 2.1 gives the frequency with which subjects were mentioned by schools, with the subjects grouped within certain arbitrary categories. Figure 2.2 presents the same information in another way, attempting to show how, according to schools' own definitions, subject areas overlap each other. In these two ways, it is hoped to provide some sort of sketchy curricular map, which would be recognizable to the average 13-14-year-old, even though some parts of it would be more familiar than others. In the first place, it was noticeable that conventional subject-labels were extensively used in many areas of the curriculum. For example, the familiar pair, history and geography, were in very good health and seemed in no danger of being swept away by social studies, humanities or other *nouvelles vagues*: 92 of the 100 schools provided history for at least some, and in most cases, all of their pupils and 93 schools were equally convinced about geography. Secondly, it seemed interesting to inquire if there was any consistency and perhaps even significance in the order in which the subjects were listed. A cursory explanation would certainly suggest some consistency existed: in particular, two staple items in the pupils' long-term diet — English and maths — were regularly placed first or second, and were provided in the curricula of all schools, only two providing different 'labels' for either of them. Core subjects like these were clearly delineated, although the type of class in which they were studied and the amount of time spent on them might vary within and between schools.[2]

Further study of the two diagrams made it possible to make some generalizations about third year curricular outlines. Nearly all schools offered some activities from each of the sections 1—11 of Figure 2.1, although not all pupils would study all the subjects in the range available at their school. In some cases, a pupil would have a chance to try several similar subjects in one section, for example craft, through a series of rotating groups, taking short turns at each activity. In other cases, certain subjects would only be available to a restricted group of pupils, for example a second language for those with 'proved linguistic ability', or woodwork only for boys, cookery only for girls. Figure 2.2 again shows the importance of the 'main' sections of the curriculum and how they are interlocked, at least in the schools' definitions of the subjects. The individual pupil can be imagined as standing in the space at the centre of all these circles, and attempting to relate to each of them. Are they all of equal value to him? What myths surround each subject? As many third year pupils prepare to make important subject choices, how will their current experience of the curriculum affect and influence them? These are some of the questions to which answers can only be sought 'on the ground', as we have tried to do for the two case study schools to be described in Part III.[3]

Some tentative suggestions about the shape of the third year curriculum can be put forward from a look at Figure 2.2. Thus some subjects seem not only to be much more clearly defined than others, but also to be easier to 'place' in the network. For example, Maths has only a minute overlap with one other subject (science), because of one instance where the two were grouped together as 'technology'. It is, therefore, almost completely a 'pure' subject and although a case could be made for relating maths closely to a number of subjects, (for example not only to science but also to technical subjects, commerce, and perhaps geography and music) there is no evidence from these data which encourages one to make these links. English, which from the outside might be thought to have close links both with the humanities and other languages, is nearly always described as a subject on its own, with drama providing the only tentative link with other subject areas. Is this the 'real' situation, or merely an artifact of the timetable? On the other hand, it was difficult to define tidily the areas labelled 'art', 'home economics' and 'technical subjects' and to allot such subject titles as 'combined craft', 'design' and 'fabric design' to one or the other. This is why these circles in Figure 2.2 overlap each other considerably. It would appear that those subjects placed clearly under the heading 'home economics' were taken in the majority of schools only by girls. Similarly, most of the technical subjects were very largely for boys only, but in Figure 2.2 the subjects were allocated to areas according to the description of content so far as this was ascertainable, rather than because of any difference in clientèle. It would of course be interesting to know how far a course named 'design' or 'use of materials' involved the planning of an integrated curriculum by, for example, art and woodwork/metalwork teachers, or whether the course name was an umbrella title for the block timetabling of several activities in these areas.

3. Systems of pupil grouping

Schools were asked to indicate what general form of pupil grouping was in operation for each year group from 11–16, and in particular whether their pupils were organized in basic teaching groups, that is, groups in which pupils would spend 50 per cent or more of their time, (Q, p. 2. no. 2). The possibilities provided for in the grid were as follows:

      (i) this year group is not represented in this school;

(ii)   the timetable for this group is not organized around basic
       teaching groups;

(iii) all basic teaching groups are drawn from the entire range of
       ability represented by this year group;

(iv)   basic teaching groups are not drawn from the entire range
       of ability represented by this year group.

The aim of this item, therefore, was to discover if pupils were in
relatively stable basic groups in the third year, and if so, whether these
groups were differentiated on the basis of the pupils' ability or not.
Words like 'streaming', 'banding', 'mixed ability', were deliberately
avoided, mainly because of the possibly spurious precision they might
provide; one man's 'banding' may be another one's 'streaming'. It was
recognized, however, that even if all respondents interpreted the rubric
in a similar way, the resulting responses would not always be
comparable. For example, a response in category (iii) from a Direct
Grant school with a highly restricted ability group, would inevitably
mean something very different in everyday teaching terms from an
identical response by a large comprehensive school.

For this analysis, only responses for the third year were recorded.
Responses from the schools are given in Table 2.4.

These results show clearly that nearly two-thirds of the schools had
some system of streaming or banding for their third year pupils.
Beyond this it is difficult to generalize, partly because a number of
these schools were involved in some form of reorganization during the
period of the study. Thus a school which could be classified for
September 1973 as 'Comprehensive' might well have a third year group
who entered the school on the basis of a selective examination, when it
was a grammar school, and had remained in the same basic teaching
groups in which they were then placed. It seemed possible that two
variables derived from the basic information questionnaire might be of
use; first, the present organization of the school in terms of pupil
selection; and secondly, the percentage of pupils in the school who
were going on to sixth-form courses, a variable on which schools
differed considerably and which would in many cases give some
indication of the nature of the school when the third year pupils
entered it. These variables were cross-tabulated with the form of third
year basic teaching group, and the results are given in Tables 2.5 and
2.6.

Table 2.6 would seem to suggest that those schools with a high
proportion of able pupils were less likely to organize their third year
pupil groups on some criterion of differential ability. In other words,
where there was a pre-selected group of above average ability it was
widely, though by no means universally, accepted that further

Table 2.4: Systems of pupil grouping in the third year

System of Grouping	Number of Schools
(ii) The timetable for this year group is not organized around basic teaching groups.	4
(iii) All basic teaching groups are drawn from the entire range of ability represented by this year group.	31
(iv) Basic teaching groups are *not* drawn from the entire range of ability represented by this year group.	64
No response	1
	100

Table 2.5: Type of school and system of pupil grouping in the third year

(ii)	*(ii)* No basic teaching group	*(iii)* 'Mixed ability'	*(iv)* 'Banding'/ 'Streaming'
Positively selective	0	16	11
Non-selective	4	8	34
Negatively selective	0	7	18

Table 2.6: Sixth-form potential and system of pupil grouping in the third year

% of pupils going on to VI form course	*(iii)* 'Mixed ability'	*(iv)* 'Banding'/ 'Streaming'
(a) 0—20%	13	39
(b) 20—50%	3	12
(c) 50—95%	15	13

'streaming' was unnecessary. It should be noted, however, that 13 of the 28 schools in this group (Table 2.6, group (c)) still divided their third year pupils in some way related to ability. Some form of streaming or banding was practised in 75 per cent of the schools in the other two categories. Table 2.5, with all the acknowledged difficulties of defining 'selectivity', tends to confirm the pattern. Sixteen of the 27 'selective' schools came within category (iii) ('mixed ability'); nearly three-quarters of both the other groups of schools (non-selective and negatively selective) organized their third year basic teaching groups according to ability (category (iv)) although, as will become clear in the next sections, methods were many and diverse.

In addition to the grid for categorizing pupil grouping systems, referred to on page 69, space was provided for respondents to comment on or explain their system of pupil grouping, if it fell into categories (iii) or (iv). (Q, p. 3, no. 2b). Examination of these comments revealed a wide variety of approaches and confirmed the suspicion voiced earlier, that the particular circumstances of each school might make comparison with other widely differing schools of dubious validity. By examining the comments in more detail it should be possible to fill in the outline provided by Table 2.4 by illustrating some of the ways in which pupils were allocated to groups. In addition, details from some schools with a highly individual approach to the question of pupil grouping may serve to highlight the problems inherent in any simple categorization of this type.

In any comparison of pupil groupings over a wide spectrum of schools, several dimensions have to be kept in mind; these would include the size of the school, the total range of ability within a school, the criteria employed for grouping and the curricular areas to which various types of grouping relate. The underlying continuum is probably seen as running from total mixed ability, (that is a pupil group which is a microcosm of the normal distribution of intelligence) to fine streaming as, for example, in a streamed Direct Grant school. In the following description, these dimensions will be borne in mind, but the respondents' comments will be grouped mainly according to categories (iii) and (iv) of the grid.

A. 'Mixed ability' grouping

It has already been shown that a minority of schools considered that their third year basic groups could be classified in category (iii) which for convenience will be described as 'mixed ability grouping'. Only seven comprehensive schools (two of which were rural schools with a two- or three-form entry) had mixed ability third year groups. Of the two large urban comprehensive schools who relied primarily on such groups, one had:

> 'House Tutor Groups. Girls are scrambled both for district and ability so there is a broad spectrum in each house.'

In another:

> '360 pupils are split into three houses of 120 each. Each house of 120 third year pupils is timetabled with a team of teachers for one

quarter of the timetable. They team teach the house in a mixed ability situation.'

Another urban comprehensive employed a somewhat similar method, allotting three mixed ability groups as one block of 90 pupils to a team of teachers who could re-divide them as they wished, thus providing for setting if they desired.

A number of schools, including one secondary modern and one comprehensive school, divided their pupils on a purely alphabetical basis; indeed this was fairly common among the comparatively large number of grammar schools and other selective schools which placed themselves in this 'mixed ability' category. In one case the process was explained in detail:

'Pupils are grouped into forms by taking the admission list which is in alphabetical order of surnames and allocating to the forms in turn, making exceptions for twins or small groups from the same school; for example:

Addis	Form X
Allman	Form Y
Bate	Form Z
Bate F.	Form Z
Beasley	Form X
Bishop	Form Y
. . . .	Form X
. . . .	Form Y
. . . . . .	Form Z'

In selective schools like this, however, where the whole year group would be drawn from a narrow band of the normal ability range, 'mixed ability' or 'random' grouping must have a different connotation from that which it would have in a non-selective school. As the head of a girls' grammar said:

'This Year Three is part of the highly selective grammar school intake but we did not stream them any further.'

Some grammar schools had other methods of forming their 'mixed ability' basic teaching groups. In one, with a three-form entry:

'The pupils choose their own groups provided they are roughly equal in number and gender.'

In another, experience in French at the primary school stage was the main criterion. In a girls' independent school, girls were placed in one of the forms according to personality:

> 'Two forms in each year — one larger than the other — for basic subjects (English, RE, History, etc.). Into the smaller form (under 20) we place the girls needing more confidence and individual handling.'

Pupils might not remain in these 'mixed ability' groups all the teaching time; several schools mentioned that setting was used for maths, or maths and languages. Other schools, selective and non-selective, might have mixed ability groups for pastoral purposes and for the teaching of some practical subjects, but have setting for what one respondent called 'all the classroom subjects'.

B. *'Banding'*

It could certainly be argued that all the selective schools described above, and those schools which made extensive use of setting, should more logically be classified with those all-ability schools, of which there were a considerable number, employing some form of banding.* Category (iv) (where the third year groups were not drawn from the entire ability range represented by the year group) embraced a wide range of pupil grouping methods from 'broad banding' to 'fine streaming' and these will be looked at in turn. Certainly one of the most common patterns was the comprehensive school with two or three 'bands' of ability, within which there were several basic teaching groups, often described as parallel or of 'equal ability'. Sometimes, as in this example, these were described as A, B and C:

> "A broad banding system is used as follows:

> | A Band | 3A1 | |
> |--------|-----|---|
> | | 3A2 | Mixed ability groups within each band. |
> | | 3A3 | |
> | B Band | 3B1 | |
> | | 3B2 | Mixed ability groups within each band. |
> | | 3B3 | |
> | C Band | 3C1 | |
> | | 3C2 | Mixed ability groups within each band. |
> | | 3C3 | |
> | | 3C4 | |

Usually, the lower band(s) had smaller classes and some provision for

---

* In the terms of the Questionnaire, in fact, selective schools *could* accurately classify themselves in the 'Mixed ability' category (iii).

remedial teaching, either to a whole group or groups, or by withdrawal of pupils. Banding might, of course, be combined with setting in some subjects, most commonly in Maths. In a number of cases it was not clear from the comments whether the groups within one band were of equal ability, although this may have been the case unless some mention of further streaming was made. In one case the explanation gave a rather different picture of 'streaming within bands':

'Seven forms graded in ability from 3_1 to 3_7. The allocation to each is based on overall ability. In maths and English setting is used. 3_1-3_4 are referred to as the top band and have a more academic timetable than 3_5-3_7, the lower band.'

Often the band was timetabled as a group so that setting or other re-grouping (for example, by sex) might be facilitated. In one school, classes were timetabled in pairs, one from the upper and one from the lower band, so that setting could take place across the whole ability range. Other arrangements were possible: the bands themselves could vary in size as, for example, in the school which had three parallel A classes, seven parallel B classes and one remedial group. A selective process could be carried out, producing:

'two groups selected on IQ score, attainment in the second form and teachers' recommendations. Five remaining groups — mixed ability, no streaming at all.'

Another example of this process in a very different context can be seen in a Direct Grant school:

'In the first year on the basis of our entrance examination one form of above average VRQ* for the school is formed, and the remaining forms are of mixed VRQ, within the range of the school. At the end of the first year some adjustments are made to preserve the pattern.'

Another form of banding was related primarily to the subjects studied, producing several groups following different courses, or at least with different ends in view. Several schools in one area seem to have had a similar system, of which this is one example:

'A system of banding according to ability is used to obtain basic teaching groups:

---

* Verbal Reasoning Quotient.

Two groups — potential O-level
Four groups — potential CSE
One group — requiring special teaching in reading and number

The system enables pupils in the fourth year to study for:

(a) a full range of subjects for O-level
(b) a full range of subjects to CSE level
(c) a mixture of both (a) and (b)
(d) some subjects at CSE level, either mode 1 or mode 3.'

In some cases the different curricula were described:

'Three ability *bands* (upper, middle, lower) with subject setting
for English, maths, science. *Upper* take French, computer studies
extra; *Lower* omit TD* and take general science (not separate
sciences) and drama extra.'

A similar system was in operation in a highly selective school:

'Third year pupils are divided into four forms, two of which
study two foreign languages. The other two forms study home
economics. The two forms studying languages are the more able
academically.'

Banding arrangements in some schools had been complicated by
changes in the school's status or organization:

'Pupils who came here at the age of 11+ as selective pupils are
grouped according to the number of languages being studied. Two
parallel groups doing French, Latin, German, one group doing
French, German, two parallel groups doing French only. The
ground covered in other subjects is much the same except for art
and craft. Pupils who came only last September from secondary
modern schools were placed in teaching groups on the
recommendation of their previous school.'

In all cases, of course, pupils had to be allotted to one or other of
the bands and this was usually done on entry, with some adjustment in
subsequent years. Specific criteria for this process were not commonly
mentioned; more often there was some reference to 'general ability'. In
areas where there had been a change to 13+ transfer, so that many
'third year' pupils had only just entered the school, several schools gave
a more detailed description, mentioning in each case the part played by

---

* Technical Drawing.

middle schools. In one, for example, there was:

> 'Banded ability based on the middle school profile and assessment plus subsequent movement after attainment testing in English and maths.'

In another school, the pupils had already been banded in the middle school, and the high school found that a broader system of two bands was preferable:

> 'A significant number of pupils "promoted" from C to B and from B to A bands as they enter the school.'

C. 'Streaming'

The question of how pupils should be selected or allotted to groups of differing ability becomes more acute in those schools where the process itself is intended to discriminate more accurately between ability groups; that is, those schools (a considerable number in this sample) who spoke of 'streaming' rather than 'banding', however much overlap there may be in practice between those terms. A good example of this overlap can be given from one school where two separate replies had been given to this question, one respondent speaking of 'bands' and the other of 'streaming'. In a small school with only two or three basic groups a 'stream' may be very similar in ability range to the 'band' of three or four parallel groups in a larger school, and there were several examples of this.

There were also examples of several types of streaming which could be described as moderate rather than rigid. It might be that there was a suggestion of fairly easy movement between streams:

> 'Pupils are allocated to teaching groups basically on ability in English. Their progress is kept under review and frequent movements are made between groups on the basis of staff reports and inspection of written work.'

In some cases, it was made clear that only some of the curriculum was transacted in the streamed groups, and that 'non-academic' subjects, for example, would be studied in non-ability groups — a situation rather similar in practice to that mentioned earlier where the 'mixed ability' groups were set for many of the mainstream subjects. One school, by the form of words used, made it seem as if the streaming process was approximate rather than precise:

> 'We tend to allocate to forms according to ability in English.'

There was, in addition, a small group of schools which made it clear that, although the current third year were streamed, the school (perhaps under a new head teacher) was moving away from streaming:

> 'The present third year groups are streamed, having come up through a system of streaming by "general intellectual ability" on entry to the school. Future third years will be unstreamed throughout and will be based entirely on social house group units.'

There remained, however, a significant number of schools where according to the respondents' own comments, a well formulated type of streaming was felt to be the most satisfactory form of grouping. It seemed as if some of these respondents thought it necessary to make their policy quite clear: 'We have no mixed ability groups'; 'Basic teaching groups are strictly streamed according to ability'; 'Six groups – streamed throughout.'

A number of these schools were non-selective, catering for a wide ability range, but two Direct Grant schools also described their third year organization in terms of streaming. Thus, in one school:

> 'At the end of two years the pupils are streamed according to the staff's assessment of their ability and suitability of pace of work for individuals. Staff meeting at the end of the second year is decisive; reference is made to examination performance as well as term's work.'

This 'fine streaming' clearly needs to be based on criteria which are as accurate and objective as possible, and some schools listed several methods which were used in conjunction for placing pupils within any given stream:

> 'The present third year was streamed on entry into the school by
>
>   (a) school internal testing
>   (b) reports from primary head teachers
>   (c) order of merit on a five point scale A to E according to primary school progress.'

It would seem, then, that among all the schools in this sample who divided their pupils into some sort of ability groups for much of the curriculum, a sizeable number not only described their method as 'streaming' but made it clear that streaming as they understood it would continue to be employed as the best form of organization for efficient teaching in their schools. In general, a study of responses from these schools has proved a useful corrective to any idea that 'comprehensive school' can be equated with 'mixed ability teaching' or that there are simple patterns of pupil grouping appropriate to one school type.

Finally, it should be added that in some schools there were selection criteria more pressing than general ability or even age, and the best example of this was a school for the deaf where the staff needed to examine first the degree of hearing-loss before allotting their pupils to the (necessarily) small teaching groups.

4. Constraints on the curriculum

In asking schools to describe the outline and context of the third year curriculum, the research team were aware that this might be a frustrating as well as a time-consuming exercise. For example, a school might be so hampered by the character and siting of its buildings that the staff would feel unable to introduce strongly desired curriculum changes, but unhappy at describing, without further explanation, the existing third year curriculum. Even if the problem were generally less acute than this, it seemed a good idea to give respondents the opportunity to mention and perhaps enlarge upon proposed changes in the curriculum, and those constraints which inhibited present intentions and future plans.

Three items were included for this purpose. Respondents were asked if the present third year timetable was in any way atypical (Q, p. 17, no. 11); if important changes were being actively considered for the third year timetable in 1974—5 (Q. p. 18, no. 13); and if the timetable adequately reflected the purposes and ideologies of their school (Q. p. 17, no. 12). Responses to those items are given in Table 2.7.

Table 2.7: Temporary and permanent third year timetable change.

	Question	Yes	No	No response
(i)	Is the third year time-table atypical?	12	88	0
(ii)	Are changes planned for 1974—5?	29	67	4
(iii)	Are there constraints on the third year timetable which you wish to mention?	57	43	0

These figures, in themselves somewhat laconic, suggest that most schools were operating in a comparatively stable situation, although nearly one-third had some changes in view. More significantly, perhaps, over half the respondents felt it worth listing the constraints which prevented the introduction of desired curriculum changes.

A closer look at the types of constraint which were mentioned shows that they fall into several well-defined groups. There were references to shortages in material resources — buildings, money and equipment; to staffing problems; to timetabling difficulties; and to curricular issues. Some of these were mentioned more frequently than others as Table 2.8 shows.

Table 2.8: Classification of constraints on the third year timetable.

	Type of problem	*Number of mentions*
1.	Shortage of material resources	35
2.	Staffing difficulties	34
3.	Curricular problems	14
4.	Timetabling constraints	9

One school, of course, might mention several of these types of constraint and the particular problem described would vary, as a few examples will illustrate. Thus within the first category, there were frequent references to inadequate or inflexible teaching space, particularly for practical subjects — 'only one woodwork room', 'lack of facilities for girls' activities', 'accommodation is very tight'. Grounds as well as buildings might be inadequate; one school had no playing field at all. Even proposed additions to buildings were not always felt to be adequate: 'there is a 50 per cent shortage in boys' craft provision due in phase three building.' Sometimes it was the inflexibility of the buildings which appeared to be the most pressing problem: 'the school is a number of self-contained boxes'. In this connection the difficulty of working on a split site was mentioned several times. In one school a move towards more integration in the curriculum, and more team teaching was felt to be impossible because:

> 'The school is on three separate sites, one site a mile from the other two. Even these two have a main road in between. A system of double lessons helps.'

In other cases, it was the general financial problem (probably felt even more acutely now than it was when these questionnaires were completed) which was mentioned, usually along with other factors, as a notable constraint on curricular development.

If problems about the material resources and facilities of the school were prominent among the concerns of many respondents, there was almost as much anxiety about the numbers and quality of the staff. In many cases, it was simply a question of teacher—pupil ratio. Twenty-five respondents in all felt that they badly needed more teachers, either to lower the overall teacher—pupil ratios or to solve a problem in one subject area. One school mentioned a ratio of 1:20; another saw the existing norm as wholly inadequate:

> We are 'adequately' staffed, but ideally the average group size should be halved.'

There might be particular reasons for the problem; an independent school felt that staffing ratios could not be improved because of the financial outlay involved. More frequently, it was a question of teachers for given subjects simply not being available — boys' craft was mentioned several times in this connection; one respondent commented: 'remedial teachers are unobtainable'. It is perhaps more disturbing to note that some respondents felt that improvements in the curriculum were hampered by the quality of the existing staff; there were references to 'uninterested' or 'uncommitted' teachers, and this raises delicate issues about the teacher's 'vocation', and the circumstances in which he works. More often concern was expressed about staff struggling to cope with curricular areas for which they were not qualified, a problem linked with the shortage of specialists mentioned above. One respondent referred ruefully to a more general problem for his staff:

> 'There is a lack of experience in mixed ability techniques among the staff (who are not keen anyway).'

Clearly, satisfaction with a staff group is a very subjective matter, and it should be said that a number of respondents commented frequently in other parts of the questionnaire on the community spirit and hard working loyalty of their staff, often in difficult circumstances. One head teacher, in particular, put this point of view forcefully:

> 'Statistically this school would appear to offer very little for boys and staff. It is, however, a friendly happy school where the majority work together in great harmony. The staff is evenly balanced between experience and youth. It is a rarity (usually due to unusual circumstances) for teachers to resign — never due to dissatisfaction. This stability we are sure has much to do with the fair discipline and friendly atmosphere upon which all visitors

comment.'*

It is perhaps interesting to note that nowhere in the responses to this item were the qualities or characteristics of *pupils* described as a constraint, a fact that might come as a surprise to the pupils themselves.

Most of the other constraints mentioned by respondents concerned particular curricular organizational problems. Sometimes the cry was simple: 'not enough time'! In one case the shortage of time was linked to an important third year issue — the options system by which subject choices for the fourth and fifth year were made:

> 'There is a lack of time during the year where the maximum number of academic subjects are taught to make possible an informed choice of options for the fourth year.'

Questions concerning the balance of the curriculum, and in particular the tension between a common core and an option-based curriculum in the third year, disturbed several respondents:

> 'The third year timetable is inevitably a compromise. Conflict between a common curriculum with stable primary groups and increased specialisation with the flexibility required, is most acute in the third year.'

Looking forward to an examination-directed curriculum meant to some respondents that external examinations were casting a shadow down to the third year courses. One school would have liked to introduce some grouping of subjects, but felt that this might not be helpful to the pupils:

> 'There are separate subjects on the timetable at present because we don't want to disadvantage pupils choosing for external examinations.'

This point was linked with the fact that pupils only had 4½ terms in this school before choosing fourth and fifth year courses. This raises another issue which concerned several respondents in schools with 12+ or 13+ entry; the difficulty of forging a link from a variety of feeder schools to a common course at the high school, leading, after a short time, to option choices. Sometimes the problem was felt most acutely in cumulative subjects like maths and languages:

---

*   This school has since merged with three others to from one mixed comprehensive school.

'Four years is not enough time for certain subjects, for example language teaching, where French in the middle school has too often led to pupils rejecting it before they arrive here.'

The problem might be seen as more general: 'Transfer at thirteen allows only one year to identify students before they enter fourth year options.' Another problem arising from a source outside the school concerned the integration of 'linked courses' (not necessarily in the third year)[4] with the school's own timetable.

Perceived constraints, then, were varied and occasionally somewhat intangible. A head teacher who felt pressed by an 'inherited staff and timetable', or tied down by the 'strong academic tradition of the school' might find these non-financial constraints just as overwhelming as the more obvious shortages of staff and resources. The force of these constraints can be examined from another angle; in an ideal world how would the status quo be altered? Responses to this question gave some indications of the variety of curricular aims which respondents set before themselves.

The most interesting point about the aims which emerged from the responses was their diversity. While constraints fell into several main types, among the ideal worlds envisaged for 13-14-year-olds there were contrasts at every level. Some were 'visionary': 'I'd like a timetable using two basic criteria: pupil needs — pupil individual preferences', while some described plans about to be implemented: 'future third years will be unstreamed as from September, 1974'. Respondents might be concerned with sweeping changes, or with particular aspects: 'I'd prefer to timetable art and music in half forms'. Even more interesting were the contrasting views expressed about some controversial issues. The clearest example concerned pupil grouping; six respondents wanted more mixed ability teaching, but six other pressed for more setting. Even where the general aim was the same — nine schools expressed a strong desire for more practical work in the curriculum — it might be related to different groups of pupils. Thus the head of one girls' school wished for more space for practical and creative subjects in the crowded timetable of the more academic students, while another stressed the need to provide the less academic with more crafts, business studies or music. There were contrasts, too, in the views expressed about the difficult question of choice in the third year curriculum — more pupil choice or a guarantee of common access to all subjects by all pupils? Both aims found their supporters.

Some of the wishes expressed here were directly related to the constraints described earlier — at least nine schools would have liked to create the more generous provision for practical work which shortages of staff and resources at present prevented. Similarly, four schools pleaded for better facilities for remedial teaching. Unrealized aims for the planned integration of subjects, for experiments in team teaching, and for schemes for out-of-school activities were all closely connected to particular constraints.

Not all respondents, of course, expressed a view of their 'ideal world' for the third year curriculum; in fact just under half of them felt it was worth making some comment. It would be dangerous to assume that the other fifty had succeeded in creating their ideal world — they may have been too busy trying to do so to write about it. It is, however, interesting that many of the desired changes were particular rather than sweeping, concerning perhaps one or two subjects which, it was hoped, could be provided for some or all pupils — music, craft and a second language were mentioned a number of times. Perhaps it is by developing one area at a time in this way, as opportunity arises, that the curriculum is changed in many schools, unless a radical change in the organization or leadership of the school provokes a revision of the whole school's curriculum.

Notes

1.   *Statistics of Education SS4, Survey of the Curriculum and Deployment of Teachers (Secondary Schools) 1965—6 Part 2: The Curriculum.* (London, HMSO, 1971).

2.   For further details, see Part III, page 110.

3.   See pages 89—104, part III, and also two other books to be published later in this series: a study of options schemes in two schools (Ann Hurman, *A Charter for Choice*) and case studies of the third year curriculum in two schools.

4.   A number of schools run courses jointly with other institutions — for example colleges of Further Education — for such subjects as car maintenance or hairdressing for which the school does not have adequate facilities. These courses are usually for older pupils, that is pupils in the fourth year or above.

PART III

*The Third Year Curriculum:
A View from the Schools*

Introductory

To the teacher in a large secondary school, historical outlines and general surveys may seem of only marginal relevance to the urgent business of organizing the work of the school for the benefit of its pupils. Indeed as soon as one becomes immersed in the life of a fairly large school it is tempting to think that its circumstances and its problems are so individual that comparisons with other schools would be worthless if not actually unhelpful. But Davies (1969) has shown that it is possible to construct models to represent the underlying reality of timetables drawn up in widely differing circumstances, and that, given certain basic ingredients (in terms of school population, length of course and work load of teachers), common ways of describing the structure of the timetable and the curriculum which it embodies can be derived and applied with profit to the whole range of secondary schools to be found in this country. Moreover, as suggested in Part I, most schools have close links with their past and with each other, and indeed past decisions may continue to reverberate in the pattern of the school's life long after the decision makers have moved on elsewhere.

Many of the 100 schools surveyed in Part II had spent recent years digesting important organizational changes, but none was an entirely new creation; in each case continuity with one or several previous schools was maintained by, among other factors, the teachers who stayed and, for one school generation, by the pupils themselves. How were these changes reflected in the structure and organization of the third year curriculum? What new trends seem to have become most firmly established and what had remained unchanged? What factors seem to have become important in finding solutions to the recurrent problems of the third year curriculum — how much choice should there be, how far should general or specific ability determine pupil groupings, how should foreign languages be provided for? And how well does the outline sketched in Part II accord with the complex reality of the school?

In order to look for answers to some of these questions, we went to two schools* and spent one school year (1975/76) working closely with them. Both schools were 'typical' in the sense that they exemplified what has been happening in many schools in recent years. But, equally, each should be considered unique. Indeed few head teachers would consider their school to be 'typical' and several replies to our inquiries in schools were prefaced by this sort of remark: 'Well, I don't think it would be much use your coming here for your study, we're hardly typical, you see, because over the last X years . . . .'

---

* Called for the purposes of this study, West Mercia High School and Victoria Comprehensive School.

In what ways, then, were these two schools 'typical'? In the first place both were comprehensive in their intake, and operated in areas where there was little or no selection within the maintained system. Both had fairly recently completed this transition to a non-selective system, and the first 'new intake' pupils were completing sixth-form courses. In both schools there were 'open' sixth forms designed to provide both for the academic pupil aiming for Advanced level examinations, and for those who wished to pursue their general education or special interests after the age of sixteen. Both were mixed schools. As it happened, both had had new headmasters within the last few years.

In other ways the schools represented different traditions. West Mercia High School was a former secondary modern school with a mixed town and country catchment area, entry at thirteen and a very large third year group. Victoria Comprehensive School, on the other hand, was a former four form entry grammar school in an urban area with pupils arriving at eleven. There were six classes in the third year of 1975/76 and in that year the school had changed to an eight-form entry. Our hope was that these two schools would exhibit enough similarities to make a common discussion possible and suggest useful comparisons. But the differences between these schools are valuable because they may point to the influence of their different traditions. Moreover, findings about the third year curriculum in these two schools (which were chosen from the 100 surveyed in Part II) can be set against information from another sub-sample of eighteen schools which contributed to the second stage of the study. In this way the type of interesting but limited close-up that results from a case study can be placed within a wider context.

The aim of this part of the book, then, is to explore in more detail some of the general issues that arose in the survey described in Part II. This exploration takes several forms: illustrations from specific cases, a closer look at some common patterns, and tentative discussion of wider issues that are raised by the evidence. The illustrations come, first, from the two case study schools; by focussing on these two schools third year issues can immediately be seen in a 'real' context, and the case study material provides some interesting instances of how these two schools approached issues which face all those planning for the 13—14 age group. Then, by looking at these two schools together with the wider group of eighteen schools, it is possible to move from illustration towards the identification of general trends and the contexts to which these are related; and to give brief examples of how other schools among the eighteen have approached these common issues. It is emphasized that it neither possible nor desirable to draw general conclusions from the experience of any one school, since the circumstances of each school, during one school year, are unique in many particulars. But, by balancing particular illustrations with evidence of general trends, it becomes possible to make some suggestions about how the framework provided by schools is related to the third year curriculum itself.

Part III begins with a short description of the two case study schools to indicate the setting of the third year curriculum there as it appeared to an observer in 1975/76. When we arrived at the schools in September 1975, we tried to establish as soon as possible a working knowledge of the third-year curriculum and organization in that school; but as we did so it quickly became apparent that it was very necessary to become familiar with their recent histories if we were to understand the significance of present arrangements. In the next section I describe how the third year curriculum structure that we observed during 1975/76 came into being, as it was explained to us by present and past members of staff at the two schools.

1. The Third Year Curriculum: two case histories
A. *Victoria Comprehensive* (see Figure 3.1)

The school, which in 1975/76 had nearly 1200 pupils, is one of a number of comprehensive schools in Blackley, a part of the West Midlands conurbation noted for heavy industry and engineering. It is a mixed 11—18 comprehensive school and is still growing in size.* In 1969 the local education authority had implemented comprehensive reorganization, establishing a number of 11—18 comprehensives, but leaving some former secondary moderns as 11—16 schools. It was in September 1969 that Victoria received its first comprehensive intake. Plans had been prepared over a long period, and when Victoria School moved to a new site in 1964 it was generally expected that it would eventually become a comprehensive school. Even so, the buildings were designed for use as a grammar school. It was decided by the planners that the school should be built in a series of house blocks. But the needs of the growing school soon outstripped these plans and by the time the headmaster left in 1973 there were seven blocks; by 1976 the number had grown to twelve, including greatly improved facilities for practical subjects. The school was built on a rather low lying site but the variety of solid brick buildings fit well together and give a welcoming, purposeful impression to the visitor, although not all of the teachers found them congenial.

The former headmaster, Mr Oliver, was proud of the academic tradition he had built up in the school; the sixth form had grown to

---

* It now (1976) has an eight form entry; the 1976/77 third year is the last to have only six classes.

200 and he felt that the school had become well known for some of its ventures in curriculum development. At the same time he felt the school was not too big for him to know all the staff and the pupils. He found the changes that followed on comprehensivization upsetting and in some ways depressing, particularly in relation to the growing size of the school. He decided it was necessary to delegate many of his former responsibilities and as a result felt isolated from much of the decision making that had once lain in his own sphere. New departments were developed to cater for some of the new intake: a remedial and a commerce department, for example. But the process of change was gradual — it was 1974 before the first non-selective intake reached public examinations in the fifth year — and it seems as if the development of new curricula or forms of organization was also allowed to take place stage by stage, changes beinng introduced when they became necessary. There was no new grand design involving wholesale redevelopment of the curriculum.[1]

In the grammar school there had been four classes in a year, two in the upper stream and two in the lower stream, called, for the purposes of this study A and B. One of the A classes was an express stream which went to O-level in four years rather than in five. But for several reasons this structure based on ability was of limited significance. Formally, it was played down, classes being named according to their tutor's initials, ('although,' said Mr Oliver, 'children always knew what band they were in whatever you called them'), and in any case pupils had many of their lessons in mixed house groups. Only maths, English and French were taught in ability groups. Before 1969 the ability of the intake had already changed because of alterations to the catchment area, and this had led staff to think about introducing CSE in some subjects higher up the school. But of course the change was much more marked with the first non-selective intake, particularly as, according to the former headmaster, 'it was such a poor intake; the curve was skewed so that there were very few people with an IQ of above 115.' Nevertheless, the same A and B band structure was preserved, with the addition of a Remedial Band (which we call 'C') containing smaller classes for the less able. The other possibility — of keeping those with learning difficulties with the other pupils and 'extracting' them from some lessons for remedial teaching — was not really considered. It seemed satisfactory at the time to group them together in a band of their own. In fact some mixed ability teaching was continued especially for the first and second year groups; this was phased out for third year pupils and for the 1975/76 third year all teaching was taking place *within* the three separate bands. The curriculum pattern for this third year group is given in Figure 3.1.

Figure 3.1: Victoria Comprehensive School; third year curriculum pattern 1975/76

Victoria Comprehensive School   186 pupils in three ability bands. 35 period week.

Class	No. of pupils	E	M	Langs.	Science	Humanities		
3A1	36	E_4	M_4	F_4Ge_3	* * *	$G_2H_2RE_1Mu_1$	A_2	B.Ch.P./B.Ch.P./B.Ch.P./B.Ch.P.$_6$
3A2	35	E_4	M_4	F_4Ge_3	* * *	$G_2H_2RE_1Mu_1$	A_2	HE/Nk/Wk/Mk$_3$
								PE/PE$_1$
								Ga/Ga$_2$
3B1	34	E_4	M_5	F_4	$B_2Ch_2P_2$	$G_2H_3RE_1Mu_1$	A_2	HE/Nk/Wk/Mk$_4$
3B2	32	E_4	M_5	F_4	$B_2Ch_2P_2$	$G_2H_3RE_1Mu_1$	A_2	PE/PE$_1$
								Ga/Ga$_2$
3C1	30	E_5	M_6		$B_2Ch_2P_2$	$G_3H_2RE_2Mu_1Dr._1$	A_2	HE/Nk/Mk/Wk$_4$
3C2	19	E_5	M_6		$B_2Ch_2P_2$	$G_3H_2RE_1Mu_1Dr._2$	A_2	PE/PE$_1$
								Ga/Ga$_2$

* means that for these subjects pupils were regrouped; groups appear on the right.

Notes: 1)   Although only C Band had timetabled drama, one A Band class had a weekly drama lesson during English.

        2)   35–45% of timetable in 'double periods'.

The curriculum pattern shows that Victoria was operating a 35 period week; a pointer to a grammar school past. (The only other schools among the eighteen to have 35 period weeks were selective schools). But Mr Oliver found that there simply wasn't room on the timetable for all the subjects he wished to cover in the grammar school and his solution was to institute a six day timetable. By 1974, the new headmaster, Mr Senior, and other members of staff had decided this was unsatisfactory in other ways and went back to a five day pattern for 1975/76. This was in fact a temporary measure, and a 40 period week was planned for 1976/77. Mr Senior was also discussing other plans which might be reflected in later curriculum change. In particular, the staff had spent many sessions in and out of school during the year considering the idea of a 'diagnostic' first term or year in which pupils would be taught in mixed ability groups for all subjects, and which would give teachers more opportunity to assess pupils fully before any decisions about banding were made.[2] But for the third year pupils of 1975/76, the context had been established under the regime of the previous headmaster, Mr Oliver, who left just before they came.

The structure on which the third year course was built was made up of *classes* placed within *bands*. It is true that pupils were also members of mixed ability house groups, but these met only for registration. For most pupils it was the teaching group, the banded class, that was the main focus; this was where they made their friends and got on with the everyday business of school life. This is not surprising when one looks at the curriculum pattern; B and C Band pupils spent 80 per cent of their lesson time in these class groups, and even the A Band, who were regrouped for science, had two-thirds of their timetabled time in their basic teaching groups. For the three science subjects (taught as separate subjects throughout the year group) the two A classes were regrouped into three parallel sets. In the A and B Bands the two classes were parallel, but in the C Band there was an explicit distinction between a more and less able group, one much larger than the other, although both groups came under the aegis of the remedial department for maths, English and history. (Several heads of department felt that the methods used with the rest of the year would be inappropriate for the C Band and the pupils there would be better off with teachers who were used to slow learners). The fact that the same teacher took a C class for both maths and English and would plan work for all nine or ten periods as seemed best at the time, marked off the C Band curriculum in these basic subjects as being rather different from the rest of the year group. There were also some clear differences in content: C Band pupils did not take French in the third year but they were the only pupils to have timetabled Drama lessons, and slightly more time was spent in the C Band than in the other Bands on humanities, maths and English. These differences reinforced the feeling that it was rather difficult by the third year to transfer to the B Band. * And a B Band member moving to the A Band after the beginning of the third year might have problems over German. At the same time, there were common syllabus outlines for many third year subjects, even if time allocations varied slightly from band to band. Teachers naturally adapted these syllabuses to the needs of particular classes and in some cases these needs were interpreted in the context of what was generally thought appropriate for a particular band.

The differences in the curriculum between the bands, which seem to have been fairly generally accepted in the school as part of the order of things, came into sharper focus when third year pupils came to choose subjects for the fourth and fifth years.[3] Here again earlier practice in the grammar school and the first years of comprehensivization had helped to shape the present. The grammar school tradition was that all pupils should carry a wide spectrum of subjects through to O-level, but some specialization was allowed for the fourth year, so that, basically, pupils were following an Arts-biassed or Science-biassed course. When the school went comprehensive it was realized that this was inadequate for the wide range of ability now coming through. In consequence, an options pattern was instituted, after much discussion, to enable A band pupils to follow more academic courses where appropriate while still allowing for a wide range of subjects for the less able. Some B band pupils might be catered for within a similar range of subjects, but aiming mostly for CSE rather than O-level. The problem was what should or could be provided for the C Band and the less able B band pupils? This, explained Mr Oliver, was where the enlarged practical departments came into their own, and a whole range of new courses was developed. By 1976, the range of options offered to third year pupils in the well prepared Options Booklet was impressive: 33 altogether, many of them at two or three levels.[4] Every effort was made in the school to see that each pupil received adequate advice and help in making the choices. But not only were some choices pre-empted by earlier decisions — French (but not European Studies) was ruled out for C Band pupils, and German (but not European Studies) for the B Band — it also seemed to the observer that many of the courses had been developed with a particular band in mind and this resulted in a tendency to steer pupils towards 'appropriate' courses. However, this is a complex subject and is only mentioned here because of the way in which the gradual change from grammar school patterns seems to have shaped the opportunities of third year pupils.

The recent history of Victoria School offers one illustration of the shaping of a curriculum framework after the transition from a selective to a non-selective intake. West Mercia High School, with the obvious

---

* Although in one case this had been done.

difference of a 13+ entry, presents a number of other contrasts in its
original context, its current curriculum framework and the way in
which that has developed in recent years.

B. *West Mercia High School* (see Figure 3.2)

West Mercia High School has rather fewer pupils in all than Victoria:
about 1100 pupils in 1975/76. But with entry at 13+, the year groups
are considerably larger. The third year of 1975/76, with more groups
than ever before, contained 380 pupils. The school had developed from
a well established secondary modern serving the town and some nearby
villages. The county education authority had been discussing plans for
reorganization of secondary schools since the early 1960s and the
decision was made to go for a three-tier system of first (5—9), middle
(9—13) and high schools (13—18). West Mercia was to be one of the
first of these high schools, fed by two (later three) middle schools.

In 1968 the previous headmaster, Mr Rutherford, had been
appointed to supervise the complex procedure of change in status, age
of entry, size and site; a new building had originally been scheduled for
1969, but the move eventually took place in September 1971, amid all
the predictable confusion of half-finished areas and deferred specialist
rooms. There was no intake in 1969 or 1970, so the first 13+ intake
(ten forms) coincided with the move to new buildings. It was therefore
1974 before the high school could produce its first crop of public
examination results that fully reflected all these changes, and it was at
this point that the headmaster retired, with the 'new' school firmly set
on its course. Looking back, Mr Rutherford felt fairly happy with the
general atmosphere in the school and the academic standards of the
most able, the 'newcomers' to the school; he also thought the school
had a good reputation for helping the less able. He saw one of the main
tasks of his successor to be the expansion of the small but thriving sixth
form, which he had begun in 1968.

The school now stands on the outskirts of the country town,
Elmsworth, which has increased considerably in size since it was
designated as a growth area, and from which most of the pupils come.
An appreciable number also arrive in buses from the countryside
around — an important point when out-of-school activities are planned.
The modern modular buildings are pleasantly laid out on an extensive
site which has been attractively landscaped. Since 1971 some further
practical rooms have been completed, and other specialist facilities are
planned. The social and pastoral side of school life is run on a house
system — four houses (North, South, East and West) for all third,
fourth and fifth year pupils.

Any 13—18 high school will have certain characteristics which set it
apart from schools with an 11+ entry. In relation to the curriculum, it

means that *if* the customary pattern, of offering a wide range of choice in the fourth and fifth years, is employed, there is only one year of 'general education' before this. Moreover this is a year in which some time will be spent by pupils and staff getting to know each other and sizing up potential and opportunities. The smoothness with which this settling in is achieved will depend to a considerable extent on how close the relationship is with the feeder middle schools, which would be true about any transition but is all the more important when there are only three years of compulsory education left. Mr Rutherford and his staff had borne this in mind in developing plans for the new school and they worked in consultation with the middle schools, particularly over syllabuses in the cumulative subjects like science, maths and French. But with all the changes that had to be digested in a fairly short time, and the particular, and novel, issues facing a 13+ school, it is not surprising that the curriculum organization underwent several major changes in the first seven years, a process which still continues. It makes an interesting comparison with Victoria, where despite the increase in size and the reorganization, the overall impression is one of continuity and stability. As one of the senior staff at West Mercia said in 1975:

'We have always been in a position where we're expanding, getting lots of new staff; the buildings have changed a bit and we can always set up something and say: "Well, we'll see how it goes, and if we don't like it we'll change", and that's been our biggest enemy I think — that we've never really carried out what we want properly in certain areas because we've always had this sort of escape hatch, "well, if we don't like it after twelve months we can change".'

The curriculum plan that was drawn up for the new school envisaged an upper band containing 60 per cent of the ability range and aiming for public examinations. The lower band (40 per cent) contained the potential early leavers, who before the raising of the school leaving age in 1972 would, of course, have left at the end of the fourth year. The bands were divided for timetabling purposes into two equal sized blocks, to facilitate block timetabling.[5] It had already been decided that the timetable should be blocked as much as possible so that departments could make their own plans about how the time should be used and the pupils organized within the given framework. The content of the curriculum was to be seen in the form of broad subject areas as much as possible, with fairly equal time allocations. With some allowance for variations between bands and years the picture was something like this:

English	5/6
Maths	5/6
Science	7
Social Studies	7
Practical	8/10
French	3/5
PE/Games	3

40   periods

Within each of these areas a number of different courses were to be developed for separate groups of pupils. This pattern, beginning in the third year, was to be carried through to the fifth year, with virtually no options of the now conventional type. As a result of his experience of secondary schools, Mr Rutherford was against options of this sort:

> 'I think once you start options you get exclusions by choice and you get exclusions, I think, by staff pressure. The child may in fact choose the wrong subjects and therefore exclude himself from an experience which may be valuable later on. But I think even more serious is the fact that once you have options . . . you're left with a number of children that nobody wants, as it were, and these children are pushed into any particular groups on sheer expediency; rather than have that situation arise I tended to have no options, but I encouraged options *within* the subject.'

During his time at the school, plans were made for integrated courses in two of the subject areas, Science and Social Studies. The new upper band intake of 1971 began straight away on an adapted version of the Schools Council Integrated Science Project (SCISP); West Mercia was one of the first comprehensive schools to try this out with a wide ability range — it had originally been designed for grammar school pupils. It was intended that SCISP should provide one part of a spectrum of science courses; there was also to be CSE integrated science and a number of 'biassed' science courses with a technological base for the less able. Similar plans were worked out for the Social Studies area, and a new integrated Mode 3 O-level course was prepared and accepted by one of the GCE Examination Boards. Incipient faculties were also being developed, grouping together the staff working on these schemes. But meanwhile other issues had arisen which were to disturb the underlying framework.

One of these, in 1971 a cloud no bigger than a man's hand, but soon large enough to cast long shadows, was the second language question. Pupils arriving at the school in 1971 were the first not to have sat the

11+ examination — they had spent the previous two years in the newly formed middle schools, where they had begun to learn French. Parents of those who, under the old system, would probably have gone to grammar school were anxious to know what provision there was for learning a second foreign language at the high school. Arrangements were made for some to learn German. Before the next year's intake was due, it was apparent that demand for this provision was increasing. So it was decided that one of the two five-class blocks in the upper band, whose timetable patterns hitherto had been identical, should include all those who wished to take a second language. These pupils would have only four periods of practical subjects instead of eight like those in the other block. The reason for grouping all these pupils in one block was a timetabling one:

> 'The practical people required blocks of time, language people required contact every day, and it was virtually insoluble.' (Mr Napier, Senior Master).

Mr Napier, who as head of the maths department was then responsible for 'piecing together the jigsaw', that is working out a timetable which would implement the plan decided on by the headmaster and senior staff, found that this two-block solution was preferable to the *ad hoc* arrangements of 1971/72, which, he felt, had resulted in 'a wretched timetable'. He explained in more detail the design of the new system. The weaker pupils who would need special help were placed in the H Band. All the rest of the intake were split into two groups of approximately equal numbers. One group contained the pupils who had chosen to take a second language [the W Band]; pupils in the other group had chosen to spend more time on practical subjects [the M Band].[6] The intention was that there would be able pupils in both bands. (The groups were known as 'bands' from the outset.) But it soon became clear that the W Band 'was classed as the better one' and this had unforeseen consequences. Mr Napier got the impression that middle school pupils were choosing to do Spanish or German for a year just to get into what they and their parents considered to be the 'better' band.

When I discussed this with Mr Rutherford, he pointed out that if, as seemed advisable, the second language option was restricted to those who had done resonably well in French at the middle school these were likely to be the more able pupils in general and this tended to result in an 'upper band sort of atmosphere'. But he, too, thought that in some cases pressure from the parents had contributed to the 'skew distribution between the two bands':

> 'The parents had certainly pressed for a second language if they

could possibly get it; this was the status symbol, because they knew grammar schools did Latin and therefore "if you can get my child into the Latin group or the Spanish group then he's going to get nearer to an approximation of a grammar school education . . ." In fact people weren't opting for a second language because they wanted a second language, they were opting for what *they thought* was a grammar school course.'

By 1975, when the research team became closely involved with the school, the third year was still divided into these two 'equal' bands and one smaller 'special' band (see Figure 3.2) and the senior staff took care to speak of 'transferring' pupils between bands; but in casual conversation some might slip into using a vertical metaphor, with movement 'up' and 'down' between W, M and H bands. Most new members of staff saw no confusion: it was widely assumed that there was a top, middle and bottom band, and one probationer even thought the five classes were streamed within the band, as well, when in fact great care was taken to try to ensure parity between the class groups. For another teacher, new to the school, the difference between his W and M classes was an empirical discovery; after he had explained how the W class were generally brighter but the M class were in many ways more rewarding to teach because of their greater enthusiasm, he was asked if he had expected this difference in ability:

'At the beginning of the year . . . no. I'm still at that phase in my career when I still expect them to know more than they do and I have to sort of keep on holding myself in and say, come on, you're expecting too much of them, really. So really I think I expected them both to be W [i.e. "top" bands] and I've had to learn quite quickly to tune down to the M band.'

So in a matter of six years a framework which had been carefully constructed to give a common course in the third year, tempered by the flexibility given to departments by timetable blocking, had undergone something of a change of use as a result of attempts to solve the second language question. One other factor had reinforced the idea that the band structure was related to general ability. At the end of the third year some departments were anxious to distinguish potential O-level and CSE groups before embarking on fourth year courses. The result of this re-sorting process was the creation of two bands now explicitly based on ability, but since, broadly speaking, the upper one would contain a majority of former 3W pupils and the second would be mainly 3M, the same initials were retained — 4W and 4M. It is not surprising that for many the structure for both year groups was assimilated to the familiar pattern of bands based on general ability.

Meanwhile, there had been another shift of emphasis in relation to fourth and fifth year courses that was to have its influence on the third year curriculum. There had always been different views about the original policy, for *courses* rather than *options* in the upper school, and as the first 'new' intake reached the fifth year a number of the staff became concerned about its practical implications. If pupils were to be examined in integrated courses it was only fair that they should be able to get more than one pass; O-level SCISP, for example, was counted as two subjects and pupils could achieve one or two passes. But the schemes for integrated courses had not been carried through exactly as projected, and the result was that many pupils in the two upper bands were carrying up to ten subjects through to public examinations; even if SCISP accounted for two of these 'subjects', some teachers felt this was too heavy a load for many children. And the new deputy head teacher, Mr York, was strongly in favour of options, on principle: a pupil was likely to be much more highly motivated towards a subject he had chosen himself, and only with an options system was it possible to provide for subjects which could not be accommodated in a 'common course' structure. So from 1974 moves were made to 'open the curriculum up' and introduce some options at the end of the third year. By 1976 the only examination subjects remaining in the fourth year 'core' were English, maths and science, although with English and science both counting as 'double' subjects for examination purposes this still added up to five potential examination passes.

Now the humanities subjects — geography, history and religious education — which in practice had had linked rather than integrated courses for most fourth and fifth year pupils, could be seen as individual subjects up for choice at the end of the third year.* In fact, the seven periods allotted to social studies in outlines of the third year curriculum (like that on page 96) had always been taught as separate subjects during that year, with each subject having the 'extra' seventh period on a rota basis. Now the new head of history, for example, who was quite happy with an options system, could develop a third year history course that embodied what he considered to be the important aims at that stage. To quote the history syllabus:

'The majority of pupils arriving at the high school have not been taught history before as a separate discipline . . . It is the aim of

---

*   All pupils would have to include one of the humanities among their options; in the fourth year, in addition to history, geography and RE there was also a social studies course with an element of work experience outside the school, and this could be chosen instead of history/geography/RE.

the history staff therefore to be not only instructive but also entertaining in their teaching of their subject in the hope that they will arouse sufficient interest in their pupils to ensure plentiful recruitment for CSE and O-level courses in the fourth and fifth years . . . If the children enjoy their history lessons then they will tend to want more and choose the subject as one of their options.'

It should not be thought that the anomalies that had crept in to the third year curriculum had got their unnoticed, or were not the cause of concern. The new headmaster, Mr Scott, who had taken office in 1974, had spent the first year taking stock and during the period of our study in the school was working out, in consultation with senior staff, the changes that he considered necessary in the overall strategy for the school. As a result a considerable amount of time and effort during the first part of 1976 went into re-thinking the organization of the third year structure, so that things were going to look rather different for the next intake. But before glancing at these later proposals it would be advisable to get a clearer picture of what was offered to the third year group that we studied. (See Figure 3.2).

It may be best to start by explaining what the diagram does *not* show. Each pupil belonged to a tutor group; for this year group there were sixteen tutor groups in all, four in each of the four houses. This was the pupil's base for pastoral and administrative purposes, and the head of house would carry the main pastoral responsibility for all its members. Thus, asked which 'form' or 'class' he belonged to a pupil would state his tutor group (for example 'S32', South house, third year, tutor group 2) and would have to be pressed to say what teaching group he belonged to (for example 3M3) because this was not seen by pupils or staff as any kind of 'identity group'.

But for teaching purposes, the class groups indicated on the diagram became very important. All pupils would spend about half their timetabled week in these class groups; for H Band classes it would be considerably more than this (29 periods out of 40). In the W and M bands maths and French were taught in ability sets; so was German. For practical subjects, W Band pupils, with only four periods, were regrouped across the band. Separate groups of boys and girls (about 18—20 in each group) spent one term in as many of the practical areas as possible. In practice, woodwork, metalwork and rural crafts were confined to the boys' groups, needlework and home economics to the girls'; but both boys and girls would probably do art and rural studies at some point in the year. For these practical subjects the M and H bands, who had seven periods, were combined, and groups contained pupils

Figure 3.2: West Mercia High School; third year curriculum pattern, 1975/76.

West Mercia High School

381 pupils in two upper bands and one lower band. 40 period week.

Class	No. of pupils	E	M	Lang.	Science	Humanities		Options
3W1	28	E_5	*	*	S_7	$G_2H_2RE_2Mu.Dr_1$	} F/F_5	$M/M/M/M/M_5$ ⎱ $Ge/Ge/Ge/Sp/ClSt_5$ ⎰ $C/C/C/C/C/C/SpecMu_4$ ⎱ $PE/PE/PE/PE/PE/PE_1$ $Ga/Ga/Ga_2$
3W2	30	E_5	*	*	S_7	$G_2H_2RE_2Mu.Dr_1$	} F/F_5	
3W3	29	E_5	*	*	S_7	$G_2H_2RE_2Mu.Dr_1$		
3W4	29	E_5	*	*	S_7	$G_2H_2RE_2Mu.Dr_1$	} F/F_5	
3W5	29	E_5	*	*	S_7	$G_2H_2RE_2Mu.Dr_1$	}	
3M1	32	E_5	*	*	S_7	$G_2H_2RE_2Mu_1Dr_1$	} F/F_5	⎱ $PE/PE/PE/PE_1$ $Ga/Ga/Ga_2$
3M2	33	E_5	*	*	S_7	$G_2H_2RE_2Mu_1Dr_1$	} F/F_5	$M/M/M/M/M_5$ ⎱ $PE/PE/PE/PE_1$ $Ga/Ga/Ga_2$
3M3	31	E_5	*	*	S_7	$G_2H_2RE_2Mu_1Dr_1$		
3M4	31	E_5	*	*	S_7	$G_2H_2RE_2Mu_1Dr_1$	} $F/F/F_5$	$C/C/C/C/C/C/C_3$ $C/C/C/C/C/C/C/ClSt/SpMu_4$
3M5	30	E_5	*	*	S_7	$G_2H_2RE_2Mu_1Dr_1$	}	
3H1	27	E_5	M_5	$EuSt_4$	S_7	$G_2H_2RE_2Mu_1Dr_1$	} $PE/PE/PE/PE/PE_2$	
3H2	18	E_5	M_5	$EuSt_4$	S_7	$G_2H_2RE_2Mu_1Dr_1$	} $Ga/Ga/Ga_2$	
3H3	18	E_5	M_5	$EuSt_4$	S_7	$G_2H_2RE_2Mu_1Dr_1$		
3H4	16	$E.M. / E.M._{10}$		$EuSt_4$	S_7	$G_2H_2RE_2Mu_1Dr_1$		

Notes:
1) Setting by ability for French and maths in W & M bands. Craft in small boys or girls groups.
2) W band have alternate weekly lessons of music and drama.
3) Craft includes art, metalwork, woodwork, home economics, rural studies, rural craft, needlework. These are studied in rotation.
4) 30% of the timetable is in 'double periods'.

from both bands. Otherwise, the timetable arrangements were much the same for the two upper bands, except that W Band pupils only had time for alternate weekly drama and music lessons, whereas the M Band had one period of each. Nor were there any marked differences in the courses taught to the two bands; in all subjects there would be a common syllabus, and in some cases (science, for example) this was highly structured so that it was important for all classes in both bands to keep in step with each other. For the H Band, however, there were a number of differences. To start with, these pupils followed a European Studies course instead of French. Although this contained a small language element, it would be hard work for any pupil who was transferred from the H Band to catch up with a class who were following a full French course. What is not obvious from the curriculum outline is that there were also marked differences in science; although the H Band also had seven periods of science, they were following a general science course (based on the Scottish integrated science programme) quite distinct from SCISP. This led some teachers to query whether these pupils really needed as much as seven periods of science, and the point came up for discussion a number of times. The other difference about the H Band relates to grouping; the four classes in the band were graded by ability (H1, H2/H3, H4) on the basis of middle school reports and internal screening. The top class in the band were considered to be potential CSE candidates and many teachers thought that some of these pupils were more able than a number in their M classes. Certainly class H1 had the advantage of being a slightly smaller group (27) than classes in the M Band. The fourth class (H4), was counted as 'remedial' and pupils were split into two small groups for their ten periods of English and maths, for both of which each group had one teacher. This was a new arrangement in September 1975; previously remedial help had been given by 'extracting' pupils from other lessons.

For subjects where there was regrouping across one or two bands the timetable was, of course, blocked; but other pressures had eaten into any more general timetable-blocking design for the third year, and even where a subject *was* timetabled for the whole band it did not follow that this would lead to a change in grouping or teaching patterns; teachers might well consider this was not feasible or useful. Thus in science, one single period out of the seven, which was blocked for the W Band, was used to show the whole band a scientific television programme in the theatre, but at other times classes were generally taught separately even if the time was blocked. Constraints within the modern languages department meant that sets were in groups of two or three, and this gave Mr Napier the option of timetabling French to fit these groupings rather than having to block it right across a band. The fact that history, geography and religious education were now clearly subjects in their own right meant that any pressure there might have been to provide a social studies blocking of time had disappeared. The third year timetable was rather evenly divided between single and double periods, and this gave it a fairly complex appearance, and led to much movement around the school which it was generally felt should be reduced.

The general pattern for the third year in 1975/76, then, followed in outline the original design for a common course for the majority of pupils except in the second language area;* but the apparent, if unintended, shift towards ability banding might have a distorting effect on the way in which this curriculum was carried out. At the same time a different kind of worry was being expressed by some teachers: that the wide range of ability, particularly in some M Band classes, was making it difficult to cater adequately for the needs of all pupils. These two pressures played their part in the restructuring of the third year curriculum pattern that was carried out during 1976, to come into operation for the next school year.[7] Briefly, these plans were to result in two explicitly parallel blocks, each containing two second language sets (not classes), and a smaller H Band for about 15 per cent of the intake. Within the two large blocks, each containing six classes, there was to be more extensive setting. Pupils would be taught in maths sets for science, and the sets drawn up for French would form the teaching groups for English, history, geography, religious education, music and drama. It was also decided that the new third year intake would study separate sciences instead of SCISP, a decision which would be reviewed after a year. When we left the school in July 1976 the implications of these changes had yet to be discovered, but it certainly seemed that within the parallel blocks there would be a much greater measure of ability grouping than there had been before.

Mr. Scott, the headmaster, in looking at the general strategy for the school explained how he understood the concept of the common curriculum – not only in the third year, but right through to sixteen:

'Ultimately – and it must be a gradual evolution – I would like to get to the position where the end of the educational process is a child who has had experience in all the fields to equip him for life.'

---

* The original plan, drawn up under Mr Rutherford, was for 60 per cent in the 'upper' and 40 per cent in the 'lower' band; in fact in 1975/76 only just over 20 per cent of pupils were in the H or 'lower' band. A slightly larger number had begun the year in this band, but there had been a number of transfers between bands during the autumn term.

This would include courses in English, maths, science, craft, and the humanities, but not the same course for all. Rather like Mr Rutherford, he wished to:

> 'be able to allot a block of time to each area of experience and delegate the planning within this to the departments concerned.'

But in a high school like this one, the third year should, he thought, be seen as a diagnostic year and a time when pupils were able to sample as much as possible of what the school had to offer. He hoped that the restructuring of the third year curriculum and the forging of closer links with the middle schools would make the diagnosis more precise and make it easier for pupils to enjoy a full range of experience during the year.

2. The case study schools in context
A. *A common curriculum for the third year*

Both these schools had arrived by different routes at some common curricular destinations for their third year groups. In neither school was there a totally common course for *all* pupils, but in both there was a common core in terms of subjects taught and the time allotted to them. In both schools, third year pupils spent a considerable amount of time in classes with others who were considered to be of broadly comparable ability, although this was more closely defined and applied to a larger part of the week at Victoria than at West Mercia. In both schools pupils were preparing during their third year to choose from a much wider range of subjects which would be offered in the fourth year, so that in some sense the third year could be seen as the end of a foundation course; although at West Mercia most of this had taken place at the middle schools. For both groups of third year pupils it was only in the area of modern languages that there was clear differentiation, with some pupils taking a second language (and some having little or no foreign language study). But while the third year curriculum structure at Victoria seemed fairly stable and accepted, at West Mercia significant changes were being proposed for the third year. Even here, however, there is an unexpected point of similarity; both staff groups were deeply involved in discussion of a 'diagnostic period' for all pupils on entry to the school, but of course it was only at West Mercia that this referred to the group of pupils with whom we were concerned.

On many of these issues we had also received information from the eighteen schools which had been selected to represent the original group of 100 schools.[8] By using this information, findings about the two schools can now be set in a wider context. The basic characteristics of all twenty schools (the two and the eighteen) are given in Figure 3.3,

Figure 3.3: Characteristics of twenty Stage Two Schools 1975/76

1975/76	SIZE	SEX OF PUPILS	AGE RANGE 11 12 13 14 15 16 17 18	TYPE OF INTAKE (SEPTEMBER 1975)	STATUS IN 1970
ELM	500–900	GIRLS		Selective (positive)	Grammar
YEW	900–1100	GIRLS		Selective (positive)	Direct grant grammar
BEECH	0–500	BOYS		Selective (positive)	Grammar
CEDAR	900–1100	BOYS		Selective (positive)	Independent boarding
WILLOW	1100–1600	MIXED		Comprehensive (from 1975)	Grammar
OAK	500–900	MIXED		Comprehensive	Grammar
ASH	500–900	MIXED		Comprehensive	Secondary Modern
WEST MERCIA	1100–1600	MIXED		Comprehensive	Comprehensive (Sec. Modern 1968)
PINEWOOD	1100–1600	MIXED		Comprehensive	Comprehensive
HAZEL	1100–1600	MIXED		Comprehensive	Comprehensive
SYCAMORE	1100–1600	GIRLS		Comprehensive	Comprehensive
LIME	1100–1600	MIXED		Comprehensive	Comprehensive
REDWOOD	900–1100	MIXED		Comprehensive	Comprehensive
VICTORIA	1100–1600	MIXED		Comprehensive	Comprehensive (Grammar 1968)
POPLAR	900–1100	MIXED		Selective (negative)	Secondary Modern
HAWTHORN	500–900	MIXED		Comprehensive (from 1975)	Secondary Modern
HORNBEAM	500–900	MIXED		Comprehensive	Comprehensive
ROWAN	500–900	MIXED		Comprehensive	Secondary Modern
HOLLY	500–900	MIXED		Comprehensive	Comprehensive
MAPLE	0–500	MIXED		Comprehensive	Secondary Modern

where pseudonyms are used throughout.

All the information used here relates to the school year 1975/76, and since a number of schools were still in a period of transition towards a fully comprehensive reorganization, the circumstances of that particular group of third year pupils may have been unique. For some schools there had been marked change since the Timetable Questionnaire was completed (May 1974); Willow School, for example, had become comprehensive; Hawthorn School, orginally an 11–16 secondary modern school, had over a period of years changed its age of entry, its (real) name and its status to become a 12–16 comprehensive school. In both these schools, however, the third year pupils had entered when a selection procedure was in operation, and to that extent were part of the old order, at a time when the staff were understandably planning for change; thus a letter from Willow School outlining the third year curriculum organization commented that a major curriculum revision was planned for the next year's third year which would be a comprehensive intake. Even in schools which were outwardly stable, extensive internal reorganization might be carried out or planned; at the end of the Timetable Questionnaire for Sycamore School there had been this note:

'Please note that the comment on the previous page [outlining plans for the year 1974/75] indicates that this year's 13–14 timetable will become obsolete.'

By looking at the timetable arrangements for the third year in 1975/76, it could be seen that many of these projected changes had in fact been carried out. So here was a school which was engaged, like West Mercia was to be one year later, in a major revision of the third year curriculum structure.

In Figure 3.3 the two case study schools – West Mercia and Victoria Comprehensive – have been placed with groups of other schools which they resemble in some easily ascertained way. For instance, West Mercia High has been placed with the two other 13+ high schools, and Victoria Comprehensive is grouped with other schools of comparable size. The schools with a selective third year group in 1975/76 formed another group. This was simply a very rough and ready grouping which could easily be challenged on several counts; the aim was to assist the reader in taking in the variety of schools included, and the schools will be listed in the same order in other tables.

How did the two case study schools compare with the rest in the outlines of their third year organization and timetable structure? In Figure 3.4 which is a kind of supplement to Figure 3.3, a brief checklist is given of the more easily described features of the third year

Figure 3.4: Third year timetable organization in twenty Stage Two schools 1975/76

	Size of third year	Timetable cycle (days x periods)	Percentage in double periods (60–80 mins)	Form of third organization
ELM	90	5 x 35	25	Parallel classes
YEW	128	5 x 40	15–20	Two second language classes and two other classes
BEECH	30	5 x 35	33	One class
CEDAR	144	5 x 36	25	Parallel classes
WILLOW	159	5 x 40	35	Parallel classes
OAK	273	5 x 40	30–40	Bands
ASH	206	5 x 40	75–90	Bands
WEST MERCIA	381	5 x 40	37–40	Bands
PINEWOOD	343	5 x 40	45–55	Bands
HAZEL	318	10 x 40	100	Bands
SYCAMORE	334	5 x 40	100	Blocks of classes
LIME	360	5 x 40	90	Blocks of classes
REDWOOD	329	5 x 25	100	Bands
VICTORIA	186	5 x 35	35–40	Bands
POPLAR	230	5 x 40	93	Bands
HAWTHORN	150	5 x 40	40–55	Parallel classes
HORNBEAM	170	5 x 40	45–50	Bands
ROWAN	114	5 x 40	60–70	Parallel classes
HOLLY	120	5 x 40	35–50	Bands
MAPLE	30	5 x 40	not known	One class

curriculum structure. While the majority of schools had a 'conventional' 40 period week, with a mixture of single and double periods, at least three operated in practice in 'double' units of at least 70 minutes for all or nearly all the third year timetable, combined in the case of Hazel School with a ten-day timetable cycle. Redwood School had changed since 1974 from a 35 period week to the 25 one hour periods noted here. Diversity in forms of pupil organization is masked here by the blanket term 'banding'; it has been pointed out in Part II that this can be interpreted in various ways, and it will be shown later that for these twenty schools, banding (as we have already seen from the description of the two schools) is a theme with many variations. On the other hand even in this diagram it is clear that one or two large schools — Lime School for example — had approached the question of pupil organization from another angle, dividing the large year group into house blocks and tutor groups for teaching purposes.[9] Two of the eighteen schools had only one third year group, so that concepts like banding were irrelevant. In fact there was a wide range in the size of the third year groups, West Mercia School, with 381 third year pupils, have the largest group of all. The third year at Victoria, by contrast, fits into a middle group of between four and seven classes.

Whatever the difference between individual schools, the central issues of the curriculum remain much the same. For the third year, perhaps the most important is the question of the common curriculum, and how that should be interpreted. This raises thorny problems of definition: what is meant here by 'curriculum', and in what sense can it be common?

Innumerable definitions have been offered for this word 'curriculum' each reflecting the author's particular standpoint, but it is not easy to discover a consensus. For instance, in a higher education context the curriculum has been described as:

'. . . a rough and ready bargain between what faculty members are willing or prepared to teach and what a sufficient body of students are willing or prepared to learn.'[10]

One general definition speaks of curriculum as:

'that inquiry that explores how conceptions of education might be enacted within the realities of schooling.'[11]

Another writer considers the school curriculum difficult to define, but concludes that:

'. . . it deals with questions of what items of content or skill or experience to include in the educational programme.'[12]

This last definition seems to be nearer to the way in which many teachers whom we have met think of the curriculum, although it is not a word they may readily use. Our observations in the case study schools suggested that apart from those senior teachers who had responsibilities for planning the work of the school as a whole, most of the teachers considered their commitments (which might be very heavy) to be more particular: to their own subject, to some aspect of pastoral care or administration, to the social and cultural life of the school. Most new secondary teachers, whether they are graduates or not, come to a school to teach the subject in which they have themselves specialized, and that is naturally their prime concern, especially in the first year of teaching. But more experienced teachers can also be so dedicated to their subject that they remain somewhat detached from the rest of the curriculum except when it impinges on their own concerns. Every head of department knows the territorial infighting that can follow from a suggestion that one subject should should gain or lose a period in some timetable reshuffle, but how possible is it for those engaged in teaching to look at the curriculum in the round? It is our experience that many teachers who are not heads of department have not had occasion to think about the whole curriculum either for the school or for a single year group, and find it difficult to stand back and see it as a whole. During interviews with English, science and art teachers in the two case study schools we showed them an outline of the third year curriculum; the following response was typical of many:

'Well, this is the first time I've seen this. I haven't really summed up the third year curriculum . . . I'm not sure that my subject deserves X periods within that framework . . .'

but as another teacher said:

'These numbers are based on somebody's opinion of what's right and it's not so far removed from my own that I would feel that I couldn't teach within it.'

There may, then, be advantages in starting out with a limited definition of the curriculum as a programme of subjects (or courses, topics or modules) offered to a group or groups of students and scheduled to occupy certain specified amounts of time and space. In these terms, a common curriculum would be an identical programme for some specified population of students.

With this definition in mind, some comparisons can be made

between the third year curriculum in the two case study schools and that offered in the larger group of eighteen schools. As a first step, Table 3.1 was drawn up to show how much time was spent on all subjects by third year pupils in all twenty schools. For this purpose, subjects were grouped into broad areas; for example, geography, history and religious education were grouped under the heading 'humanities'. (Full details are given in the notes under the Table.) The time spent on each is given in terms of 'curriculum units'[13] each equal to one-ninth of the timetable cycle (which can for practical purposes be thought of here as one school week). A single entry for a school against one 'subject' shows that all third year pupils in that school have been given the same overall time allocation, although it could be used in different ways; for example, while all these pupils at Holly School had 1.1 units (five periods) of English, the single entry of 1.4 units for science at Poplar School conceals the fact that the top band of four classes followed an integrated science course for six periods while the other pupils there had two periods each of the separate sciences. Where two sets of figures are given, this indicates the minimum and maximum amounts of time that could be spent by third year pupils in that subject area. Very often this represents differences between the curriculum of a number of ability bands, as for example at Oak School, where, although a minority of pupils took no foreign language, others might take one, two or even three, according to which band and class they were in.

One can see from the table that some subjects are more likely than others to be given a common time allocation for all pupils. First of all, there are the 'core subjects' — English and maths — which are studied by all pupils below the age of sixteen, irrespective of age or ability. At West Mercia School, all third year pupils had five periods (1.1 curriculum units) of English and maths respectively.[14] In this arrangement the school was typical of many others in two ways. First because there was a common provision within the school; sixteen of the twenty schools had a common allocation of time in the third year for maths, and fourteen for English. (Victoria School was one of the exceptions, in that there were some variations in the time spent on both English and maths by pupils in different bands.) Secondly, there was wide agreement *between* schools about the proportion of time to be spent on these basic subjects: eleven other schools among the twenty provided 1.1 curriculum units of maths for all pupils. Except where the structure of the timetable made this inconvenient, pupils tended to receive a daily ration of maths. This may surprise no one in the schools; least of all the pupils, who had probably been accustomed to this pattern for all nine years of their school life, but in the current atmosphere of urgent concern about standards in these basic subjects it is worth underlining the stability and consensus to be found in schools about the place of these subjects in the curriculum.

More interestingly, fourteen of the schools had made a common time allocation *within* the school for the humanities area, although the variation *between* schools was greater — from 1.0 to 2.0 units. Again, West Mercia School illustrates the pattern found in many schools. Here the humanities area was divided into three subjects, with an equal share of the total time for all pupils: H_2 G_2 RE_2.[15] Other schools varied the total amount of time and the balance between subjects — for example H_3 G_3 RE_1 — but often had the same pattern for all third year pupils. Victoria School again illustrated a different approach, with humanities tailored to fit the requirements of each band, so that while the A band had G_2 H_2 RE_1, Class C1 had G_3 H_2 RE_2. One school did not include RE in the third year curriculum at all, and in another personal relationships was offered in its place. But history and geography appeared in every school, with either two or three periods allocated to each. The only integrated humanities course was at Pinewood School where the four C Band classes had six periods of social studies.

But in the time available how much detailed study could be made of each subject? What were the main aims for these humanities subjects at the third year stage? The head of history at West Mercia School had made it clear that the main purpose in those particular circumstances was to get pupils enthused with the idea and 'feel' of history. All three subjects would go into the options pool for the fourth year, to be joined by a new hybrid in the humanities area, social studies. So in the third year as at many other schools, some pupils might be studying one or two of the humanities subjects for the last time in their school career. It seems as if the inclusion of these familiar subjects in the third year curriculum may have been serving at least two purposes; to complete a basic grounding, a 'foundation course', for those pupils who would 'give up' the subject at the age of fourteen; and to ensure that all pupils had a sufficiently clear idea of the identity of each subject to enable them to make choices for the fourth and fifth years.[16] In fact the contrast between the place of humanities subjects in the third year curriculum on the one hand, and in the fourth and fifth year curriculum on the other, is interesting. At the two case study schools, in the fourth year, subjects which had been chosen as options became much more nearly equivalent in terms of time allocation to the 'core' subjects (English and maths at Victoria; English, maths and science at West Mercia). Most main subjects took up about one curriculum unit, (4 or 5 periods; 7 periods for science at West Mercia, 6 for English); any one pupil would have seven main subjects and a supporting programme of 'non-examination' activities — PE, Careers, RE and so on. This change — for example from 2 to 5 periods a week for one subject — might seem like a transformation to some teachers in the humanities

Table 3.1: Twenty schools: time allocated to subject areas in the third year curriculum.

School	English	Maths	Languages	Science	Humanities	Aesth/Pract.	PE	Pastoral etc.
ELM	1.0	1.3	1.8	1.5	1.5	0.8	1.0	—
YEW	0.9	1.1	1.1–2.3	1.4	1.6	1.1–2.0	0.5–0.7	0.2 (Library)
BEECH	1.0	1.3	1.5	2.3	1.0	1.0	0.8	—
CEDAR[1]	1.3	1.3	2.3	2.3	1.5	— see note	0.3 see note	—
WILLOW	1.1	1.1	2.0	1.4	1.6	1.1	0.7	—
OAK	0.9–1.4	1.1	0–2.8	1.4	1.6	0.7–2.5	0.7–0.9	0.2 (Careers/Library)
ASH	1.1–1.6	1.1–1.4	0–2.3	0.9–1.4	1.1	1.1–3.2	0.9	—
WEST MERCIA	1.1	1.1	0.9–2.0	1.6	1.4	1.1–2.0	0.9	—
PINEWOOD	1.1	1.1	0–2.0	1.4	1.6–1.8	0.5–1.8	0.9	0.2 (Careers)
HAZEL[2]	1.4	1.1	0–0.9	1.4	1.4	1.8–2.3	0.9	—
SYCAMORE	0.9	0.9	1.4	1.4	1.4	2.3	0.9	—
LIME[3]	1.1	1.1	0–1.8	0.9	1.6	1.8–3.2	0.5–0.9	0.2 (Tutor period)
REDWOOD[4]	1.1–1.5	1.1	0–0.7	1.1	1.9	1.9	0.4–0.7	1.1 (Pastoral, Careers)
POPLAR[5]	1.4	1.1–1.4	1.1	1.4	1.1–1.4	1.8	0.5–0.9	—
VICTORIA	1.0–1.3	1.0–1.5	0–1.8	1.5	1.3–2.1	1.5–2.3	0.8	—
HAWTHORN[6]	1.4	1.1	0.7	see note	1.8	see note	0.9	0.2 (Careers)
HORNBEAM	0.9–1.4	1.1	0–1.8	1.4	1.6–1.8	1.6–2.5	0.9	0–0.2 (Library)
ROWAN[7]	1.0–1.8	1.1	0.2–0.9	0.9–1.4	2.0	1.8	0.7	—
HOLLY	1.1	1.1	0.7–1.1	0.5–1.4	1.6–2.0	1.8–2.8	0.9	—
MAPLE	1.1	0.9–1.1	0–1.6	0.9–1.4	1.4–1.8	1.4–2.8	1.1	—

Notes:

Entries are made in terms of notional 'curriculum units', nine of which make up one timetable week.

Humanities = Geography, History and Religious Education.

Aesthetic/Practical = Music, Drama, Art, Craft, Woodwork, Metalwork, Technical Drawing, Domestic Science, Home Economics, Needlework, Pottery.

1. In this boarding school games take place outside timetabled hours; all boys take a six week art course during the year; craft subjects are organized on an individual basis outside timetabled hours.

2. There is also a remedial form whose timetable includes 14 periods (3.2 units) of integrated studies.

3. In addition to those pupils taking French and/or German some will take an Asian language or English as a second language.

4. Every class has two periods of 'pastoral' and one period for careers advice; there is a remedial form with an integrated course 'Activity' of 4.5 units (12 one hour periods).

5. This includes a remedial form who have, in addition, Lib_2 $Drama_2$.

6. All third year classes are regrouped for 9 periods, i.e. three 'triple' periods, for art, science and craft subjects.

7. This includes a remedial form who have, in addition, general studies$_4$.

area; now there was ample time to begin a thorough study of the one subject. (At the same time English teachers whose subject was to lead to a double entry at public examination might feel hard pressed with 5 or 6 periods.) So by the fourth year, each of the subjects within this area was on a par, from the point of view of time allotted, with basic subjects like maths and English whereas in the third year all the humanities subjects together might only take up slightly more of the total time than English on its own.

In science, too, many schools seem to have found it possible and satisfactory to lay down a common outline for all pupils. Here Victoria School exemplified the most widely found pattern: for all pupils there was a double period for each of three subjects, physics, chemistry and biology. Two boys' selective schools increased this to three periods for each subject for all pupils. West Mercia School, on the other hand, was the only school to provide a clearly integrated recognized science course (SCISP) for the majority of pupils although a number of schools were experimenting with general or integrated science courses of their own devising, perhaps for only some third year groups.[17]

By contrast, the greatest variations in time allocations within and between schools came in languages, and the composite aesthetic/ practical area. In the latter area, even with the inclusion of music (offered by all schools to some pupils), some pupils only received 0.5 units (2 out of 40 periods); on the other hand, there was a possible maximum of 3.2 units (14 out of 40 periods). Provision in this area varied in other ways; in type of work (art, music, separate or integrated craft subjects); whether this was to some extent determined by sex (for example, metalwork *or* needlework); the size of the group; and the range of specialist rooms and staff available. There were differences between the schools on all these points. In one or two schools the information supplied made it clear that pupils could choose freely between craft subjects, but in others the timetable itself showed that boys' and girls' crafts were organized separately. In some schools with a 'banded' curriculum, lower band pupils were given more time in this area than top band pupils. For example, at Pinewood School there was the following pattern: A Band classes, C_2; B Band, C_5; C Band, C_8. At Hornbeam School, where there were six third year classes arranged in A, B and C bands, a different approach was adopted for craft subjects. Time spent within this subject area depended partly on whether pupils were taking two languages (some A Band pupils), one language (some B Band pupils) or none (some B Band and all C Band pupils), but within the time available pupils were able to choose freely between the subjects offered. Information from the school giving the exact number for these teaching groups showed the results of this choice:

3B2/3C2 (20 boys, 35 girls)

Choice 1			Choice 2		
Art	6 boys	9 girls	Woodwork	9 boys	9 girls
or Metalwork	14 boys	9 girls or	Tech. Dr.	11 boys	7 girls
or Needlework		17 girls or	Home Econ.		19 girls

The approach to aesthetic and practical subjects at West Mercia School was rather different and was designed to fit the circumstances of 13+ entry. Thus in their last term at middle school it was explained to pupils that they would be given the opportunity to sample a wide range of practical courses during the year, before making more definite choices for the fourth year. But in practice there were several restrictions on this 'sampling' procedure. In the first place, some craft subjects were restricted to one sex, an outcome made more likely, though not inevitable, by the division of pupils into separate boys' and girls' groups for all practical subjects. Secondly, those pupils who chose on entry to the high school to take a second language (or special music) only had half as much time for practical subjects as the others; this made it more difficult to ensure that they covered all areas. Thirdly, staffing and facilities varied for the various practical subjects: for example there were three teachers and three rooms for art, and one teacher and one room for rural studies.

It was characteristic of many of the schools that foreign languages and practical subjects should complement each other. It might be a straightforward alternative, as at Yew School, a girls' direct grant school, where two classes took a second foreign language and the other two had home economics and needlework. More often, as at West Mercia, it was a question of stretching the time so that pupils covered both subject areas but for shorter periods of time. In fact, foreign language provision at the third year level can be one of the most problematic areas for those planning the curriculum. Should all pupils take a foreign language at this stage? What proportion, if any, should study two languages? How is time to be provided for minority subjects? These questions are dealt with in more details on pages 119–127.

Still thinking of the curriculum, for the moment, as a programme of subjects, it seems from the evidence reviewed here as well as the more general picture given in Part II, that there is a high degree of unanimity about the outlines of what should be studied by all third year pupils in all types of school, although some subjects are more firmly established in the canon than others. In fact, the stability of a subject may be revealed by the degree of consensus between schools about how much time should be spent on it. Only in two of the broad subject areas employed in Table 3.1 were there wide variations, with some pupils (or schools) spending a large amount of time on foreign languages and very little on craft and the aesthetic side, while others might have no foreign language study at all. On a broader perspective, most of these schools were offering most of their pupils a curriculum which would have satisfied the authors of the Newsom Report who, after underlining the need for basic literacy and numeracy, made their prescription as follows:

> 'If this report were about all the pupils in secondary schools instead of only half we should still hold that up to the age of sixteen nobody should go without some practical work, some experience in mathematics and science and some in the humanities. And it ought to be a sizeable share of each, not a concession to idealistic theory which sensible folk need not take too seriously. Up to this point we are rigorists. We would like to prescribe this for all pupils in all secondary schools as an obligation.'[18]

Interestingly, there is no reference here to the learning of foreign languages, one of the areas where there was least agreement among our group of twenty schools.

This prescription, couched in universal terms, suggests that the need for all children to follow it is somehow self-evident, or follows from generally agreed principles about the value of different forms of knowledge or experience. But at the more particular level of school subjects in the third year curriculum, the reasons why many subjects hold their place there may be more prosaic and easier to trace. For instance, the 'proper study of mankind' advocated in the Newsom Report could be carried out through a variety of programmes: in many junior and middle schools it would probably be more common to find this subject matter dealt with under labels like 'environmental studies' or 'integrated studies' than as separate subjects like history and geography, and in the first and/or second year of a number of secondary schools, humanities time might be taken up by a general course like 'Man, a Course of Study' (MACOS).[19] So why the more traditional history/geography/RE in the third year? One reason has already been suggested; that is the need to establish the identity of individual subjects before the pupils make choices for the fourth year, and it may be remembered that in Part II this was the reason explicitly given, in the questionnaire reply from one school, for not introducing the grouping or integrating of subjects in the third year.[20] There is also the argument that this may be a terminal course in a subject, for those who do not choose it as an extra option in the fourth year. In some cases it may be necessary actually to begin public examination courses in the third year, so that the change from more general programmes (humanities, general science) to the individual subjects that may later be taken for public examination (geography, chemistry) may take place at the end of the second year. In either case it may be pressures from within the school system, particularly the public examination system, that are helping to shape the way in which the very general aims outlined in the Newsom Report are translated into the subject-orientated third year curriculum.

Other pressures more remote from the immediate concerns of the school can play their part in maintaining the consensus about what subjects should be taught as well as keeping open the areas of debate. Thus tradition – in this case what could broadly be called the grammar school tradition, strongly upheld by many parents who themselves experienced it – suggests that by the third year pupils should be given the opportunity to learn a second language. Tradition of another sort holds that there are boys' crafts and there are girls' crafts, and at a time when there is a shortage of staff and facilities for subjects like metalwork and woodwork there is no great incentive to go against tradition. Parents (and pupils) if asked what should be included in the curriculum will tend to think in terms of subject labels with which they are already familiar, concentrating always on the 'basic subjects' of English and maths.

It might not be difficult, then, to secure a wide measure of agreement *between* schools about the broad subject areas that should be included in the third year curriculum of all secondary schools, and in some cases the consensus might extend to individual 'subjects'. Even with our group of twenty schools, by looking at one sub-group – the selective schools – it might be possible to get that consensus spelled out even more precisely. But those schools were providing for a sub-section of the age group, for whom there had long been a common curriculum. What about the 'common schools', the comprehensive schools , taking in all the children who presented themselves; was it possible to provide a common curriculum – still defined in terms of a common programme of subjects for pupils of all abilities – *within* the school? This was the question to which Benn and Simon (1972) addressed themselves in their survey of comprehensive schools referred to in Part I, and which seems to underlie much of the current debate about the common curriculum. Returning for a moment to Table 3.1, if a school provided a common programme for all its third year pupils this would show up as a line of single entries. On this criterion the only non-selective school to offer a common programme was Sycamore School, a large 11–18 girls' comprehensive school. The arrangements made here were interesting in several ways and I shall describe the curriculum at this school more fully later.[21] At the moment it is sufficient to point out that the third year course was planned in broad subject areas of the sort used for this table, so that for example all pupils had 1.4 units in the language area, but this time might be spent in different ways by different groups. This concept — of sketching out the curriculum in terms of 'areas of experience' for all, with differentiation within them — had been the one adopted at the outset at West Mercia School, under the direction of Mr Rutherford, the first headmaster. Although the plan was never fully realized, the outline remained in the form of common time allocations in five of the seven subject areas of Table 3.1. Another approach would be to provide a common programme defined in terms of subjects for all but a small minority of pupils, and this had been done in several well established comprehensive schools like Hazel School, for example, where all but two of the twelve classes had an identical curriculum outline.

In many other schools there were variations in the course outline because the approach to curriculum planning was that employed at Victoria School. This approach could be summarized in the following terms: within the framework of a general education, consider the varying needs of pupils; establish groups of pupils whose needs are broadly similar, and then adapt the general outline to suit these groups. Obviously there could be a common programme for all bands (as was the case at Hazel School), but there was a tendency for those variations which we have seen to be fairly common in the third year curriculum to be related to the band structure: only one band takes two foreign languages, one band spends more time than other bands on practical subjects. In this way the form of grouping may come to have an important influence on what is learned by different groups of pupils.

It seems, then, that in any school which caters for a wide range of ability there is unlikely at the third year level to be a wholly common curriculum, as we have defined it; that is, all pupils taking the same subjects for the same amount of time. There is likely to be *some* differentiation either in the subjects studied or in the time spent on them. A wholly common programme can be drawn up, under certain conditions; for instance, it may be agreed that *all* pupils should study one foreign language, and none should take two. This would immediately eliminate one set of planning problems. Alternatively, the programme can be planned as a common framework, within which different courses can be accommodated — the approach adopted at Sycamore School. In any case, even with a common programme, there is still room for many answers to the question 'Are all the pupils following the same course?' As we saw at West Mercia School, within the seven periods that all third year pupils spent on science, two courses were run: SCISP for the majority and a flexible general science programme for the H Band. In this respect, the common programme had been interpreted in relation to another set of planning decisions — about how pupils should be grouped — and two separate courses provided for pre-specified groups of pupils. So, after all, it is inadequate, even at this general level, where the complex issues of classroom experience are not under discussion, to define the 'curriculum' simply in terms of content — subjects to be studied. 'What should be taught, studied and learned' (which Walker (1973) described as the central problem of the curriculum) may be vitally affected by organizational decisions taken before the school year begins. Before looking at these general issues, it is worth taking a closer look at the arrangements for that subject area of the third year curriculum where timetabling matters can be a major consideration — the teaching of foreign languages.

B. Foreign languages in the third year curriculum *

The question of how many pupils should study a foreign language at all and, further, whether and when some should begin the study of more languages, has its roots in English educational history. As was pointed out in Part I, a norm was established early in the century for all secondary (grammar) schools: all pupils should study one language other than English up to public examination level at 15 or 16; if more than one such language was to be studied it was official policy at the beginning of the century that this should be Latin. Later it became accepted that German or some other modern language was an equally acceptable alternative. Very few pupils in the public sector outside these schools learned even one modern language, until it became the custom for the top streams in many secondary modern schools to study French, in the hope of taking it at GCE O-level in the fifth year. With the development of the comprehensive school, what was to be the place of foreign language teaching in the common curriculum recommended for the first three years? Two principal questions arise in relation to the study of language in the third year: firstly, even if all pupils have been introduced to French or some other language, is it thought sensible or profitable for them all to continue with it at this stage? Secondly, if some (or all) of the third year pupils are to aim for *two* foreign languages at O-level or CSE, is it essential or desirable for them to begin this study in the third year (or earlier in some cases)? Answers to these questions will depend on a number of factors, including the ability and interest of the pupils, the availability of specialist staff, and, as I have already suggested, the way pupils are grouped for work. In order to

---

* The phrase 'Language other than English' most accurately expressed the area under discussion; but in the text the less cumbersome if Anglocentric 'foreign languages' will be used instead.

Table 3.2: Foreign languages studied in the third year in twenty schools 1975/76

SCHOOL	Language I			Language II		
	% of third year pupils	subj/time allocation (curric. units)	no./type of groups	% of third year pupils	subj/time allocations (curric. units)	no./type of groups
HAWTHORN	100	F 3 (0.7)	5 mixed BTG			
HOLLY	100	F 5 (1.1)	3 banded BTG			
ROWAN	100	F 3 (0.7)	1 low ab.gp			
		F 4 (0.9)	3 ab. sets			
HAZEL	95	F 1 (0.2)	1 low ab.gp			
		F 4 (0.9)	10 banded BTG			
POPLAR	95	None	2 low ab.gps			
		F 5 (1.1)	8 banded BTG			
REDWOOD	31	None	1 low ab.gp			
		F 2 (0.7)	3 A band BTG			
		None	8 banded BTG			
SYCAMORE	100*	F/Ge/C1St 6 (1.4)	15 Ability sets	(?)	Some top sets took German (see note)	Ability sets
BEECH	100	F 4 (1.0)	1 (select) BTG	100	Ge/C1St 2 (0.5)	2(select)sets
CEDAR	100	F 5 (1.3)	6 (select) sets	100	L/Ge/Sp 4 (1.0)	6(select)sets
ELM	100	F 4 (1.0)	3 (select) BTG	100	L 3 (0.8)	3(select)BTG
WILLOW	100	F 4 (0.9)	6 (select) sets	100	Ge 5 (1.1)	5(select)BTG
YEW	100	F/Sp 5 (1.1)	4(?) (select) sets	50	Ge/L 5 (1.1)	2(select)sets
WEST MERCIA	100**	F 5 (1.1)	10 banded ab.sets	44	Ge/Sp/C1St 4 (0.9)	6 sets
		EuSt 4 (0.9)	4 low ab.BTG			
OAK	92	F 4 (0.9)	2 A Band BTG	12	(Ge 4 (0.9)	1 A Band BTG
		F 5 (1.1)	7 banded BTG		(L 4 (0.9)	
				12	Ge 5 (1.1)	1 A Band BTG

Table 3.2 (continued)

ASH	75	F 5	(1.1)	5 banded BTG 2 low ab.gps	31	Ge 5	(1.1)	2 A Band BTG
VICTORIA	74	F 4 None F 4 None	(1.0) (1.0)	2 A Band BTG 2 B Band BTG 2 C Band BTG	38	Ge 3	(0.8)	2 A Band BTG
PINEWOOD	73	F 5 None	(1.1)	8 ab.sets, A&B 4 C Band BTG	18	L/Sp 4	(0.9)	2 A Band BTG
HORNBEAM	48	F 5 F 5 None	(1.1) (1.1)	2 A Band ab.sets 1 B Band set 2 B Band sets 2 low ab.gps	28	Ge 3	(0.7)	2 A Band ab.sets
MAPLE	<100	F4	(0.9)	1 set	<100	Ge 3	(0.7)	1 set
LIME	<100	F/Ge 4	(0.9)	6 sets	8	F/Ge/Asian Langs 4 (0.9)		2 sets

*At Sycamore School (see Figure 3.7 for curriculum pattern) pupils might take one or more languages within the six periods. A Block of three classes might be divided as follows: Set 1 F4 G2; Set 2 F6; Set 3 F2 C1St 4; Set 4 C1St 6.

** At West Mercia 80% of third year pupils studied French; the other 20% took European Studies which included a limited amount of French language but was mostly concerned with French and European culture.

Notes: *BTG* = basic teaching group, i.e. Primary Group or other stable class unit in which pupil received a substantial number of lessons.

Banded BTG = basic teaching groups which are themselves grouped into Ability Bands.

Mixed BTG = basic teaching groups not based on ability.

ab.sets = ability sets, i.e. sets chosen according to specific ability in the language, across two or more BTGs.

low ab.gp = remedial or 'C Band' groups with a noticeably different curriculum.

sets = groups established especially for the language, but they may be based on pupil choice aptitude or other factors.

(select) = basic teaching groups or sets formed from a population which is of above average ability.

discuss the solutions found by the twenty schools, these have been grouped according to the type of language provision made in each for the third year. The information is given in Table 3.2.

The description of the curriculum at the two case study schools, and the way in which it developed, showed that the question of who should learn foreign languages and what effect this might have on other areas of the curriculum had been a central one in any planning of the third year curriculum. At West Mercia School in the early years it appeared to be a small scale issue: how to accommodate a minority of pupils who wished to take a second foreign language. In fact the creation of a 'second language band' proved to have far reaching implications for the rest of the course. At Victoria School it was quite a different problem: how to move from a context where all pupils took French, and some pupils took Latin and/or German as well as French, to one where it might be inadvisable for all pupils to continue even with one foreign language into the third year, and a much smaller proportion of the third year would profit from studying two. But the result in terms of the two schools' 1975/76 curriculum was not too different in outline: in both, about 39 per cent of the third year pupils studied two foreign languages (including the W Band Classical Studies group at West Mercia who learned some Latin), and at least three-quarters of the year group took French. Perhaps the most obvious differences were that at West Mercia there was a choice of a second language — German, or Spanish, or Latin (with Classical Studies) and, unlike the C Band pupils at Victoria who had given up French completely, the lower ability pupils in the H Band spent four periods each week on European Studies. The emphasis here was mainly on European life and culture but it included some language study, making use of the four years spent on French in the middle schools. To what extent did other schools follow similar patterns?

The *amount* of foreign language teaching in all twenty schools, in terms of time spent and the proportion of pupils studying languages, can be seen fairly easily from the Table. Ten of the twenty schools offered some kind of modern European language study to all their third year pupils, and in three other schools this was true for at least 90 per cent of the pupils. Usually the language was French. Only three schools offered a modern European language to less than half of their pupils; two of these schools were in Educational Priority Areas where for a substantial number of pupils English itself might be a second language. At one of these, Lime School, provision is now being made for some third year pupils to study a non-European language, Punjabi or Urdu for example, as their first foreign language.

The strength of French at the third year level in all types of school comes out clearly in Table 3.2. Only two schools, Lime and Yew, gave a choice for the first foreign language, and none offered a compulsory alternative to French. Clearly this is related to prior decisions about the employment and availability of specialist staff, as well as other factors. How versatile, for instance, are the members of the modern languages department? At West Mercia School, when Spanish and Latin were introduced fairly recently, a number of questions arose, and continued to cause headaches to those responsible for working out the details of the timetable. How many groups would be taking these new subjects, would they be of an economic size, how could pupils be encouraged to choose these subjects, could the teachers also teach other subjects or languages, could *their* timetables be appropriately filled? Unless a decision is made to fix on a main language other than French for the majority of pupils, all other languages will tend to come into the uncomfortable no-man's land often reserved for minority subjects. Or the curriculum may be affected by earlier staffing decisions; if, as happened at one school, a teacher already in the employ of the school can only teach Latin or Classical Studies, it may be necessary to arrange that some pupils take these subjects.

Fourteen of the schools provided some pupils with the opportunity of taking a second foreign language. There was more variation here, both in the language offered and in the proportion of pupils taking it. Among the schools with a selective third year, four expected all their third year pupils to study two languages and in the fifth school this was the case for two out of the four classes. In the other nine schools the proportion, as might be expected, was much lower; always under 50 per cent and in one as low as eight per cent. This proportion was to some extent related to the size of the school, because apart from West Mercia (six groups) and Maple (one group), all the non-selective schools had two groups, regardless of the number of pupils. At West Mercia, second language provision consisted of three sets for German, one for Spanish and two for Classical Studies. Of these two, one included Latin with some background study, while for the other group (from the M Band), there was no direct study of Latin. Choice of a second language had been made on entry from the middle schools, with a certain amount of screening on the grounds of their earlier performance in French. Additional language provision was made in another way at Oak School, where one class of pupils took three languages, French, German and Latin.

The 13—18 high schools have a particular problem which affects all sequential subjects, that is those subjects like maths and languages where each stage of learning depends heavily on what has gone before. On entry to the high school, pupils will have come from a number of middle schools, where they will have been taught by teachers who may be unknown by the high school, and whose approach may differ even when there is an agreed syllabus. It may be necessary to spend much of the first term on what is for some pupils revision of earlier work, in order to make sure that all pupils have covered the same ground. It is interesting that, given these real difficulties, there is little difference from an organizational point of view between the language provision of these schools and the rest. Indeed, two of them offer a particularly wide range of language teaching in the third year. Perhaps it is the break at 13+ which, if anything, encourages them to offer a second (or third) language as part of the new high school programme.

A certain amount of information can be gleaned from Table 3.2 about the approach to language teaching in the schools. In all but one school, language teaching took place in groups that were based in some way on ability.* The exception was Hawthorn School where all third year pupils had three periods of French in their 'randomized' class group. Where a school had a band structure, language teaching usually took place within the band; in some cases this was almost inevitable because there was a different time allocation between bands. Where there was setting, this might be arranged according to linguistic ability across the year group, as at Cedar School. More often, it was not feasible to teach the entire year group at once, and setting took place over some sub-division of it. This might represent the whole ability range of the school, or, in many cases, a limited part of it. The head of modern languages at West Mercia School explained why, in the third year, setting was confined to groups of two or three classes within a band at the most:

> 'We have tried to get all five sets in one band set right the way across . . . but because of commitments in the fourth, fifth and sixth, it couldn't be done. I suppose in a sense it depends on the composition of the department, where you have some people with their own teaching subjects.'

When a decision has been taken to group the pupils in bands according to general ability, differences in the course outline for each band are often most obvious in the area of languages. The arrangement at Victoria School illustrates this idea in a clear and simple way. In the third year two parallel A Band classes had four periods of French and three of German; two parallel B Band classes had four periods of French; and the two C Band classes had no foreign language teaching. The band structure provided easily determined and clearly understood cut-off points for both languages. Interpretations may vary as to where

---

*   In three of the 'selective' schools pupils were taught in their parallel classes, but of course the selection by ability was built into the school system.

this cut-off point should come; at Redwood School it was only the A Band who took French, and at Hornbeam the A Band were joined by one set selected from the two B Band classes, whereas at Poplar only one remedial class was excluded from French; but from the point of view of the timetable planner it is a convenient way of making the break so that the curriculum of these groups can be planned separately, without having to fit some subjects awkwardly into empty language 'slots'. This method of setting languages against other subjects is one of the two approaches open to planners in schools where languages are not studied by all. It was adopted by Lime School, where French and German were set against technical drawing and PE, or against some periods of craft. The other approach is to arrange that all pupils should make some study of European cultures, either directly through the language or 'in translation' as it were, by means of European or Classical Studies as was done at Sycamore and West Mercia Schools.

It seems clear that second language provision for a minority of pupils constitutes, in many schools, the most obvious exception to a 'common course' outline, and that efforts to accommodate it in the timetable may have implications for other parts of the curriculum and other groups of third year pupils than those taking the second language.[22] Given these difficulties, why do so many schools make this provision in the third year, when other new 'minority subjects' are often introduced later in the context of the fourth year options schemes? Within the school, and more particularly within the modern languages department, the explanation may be on these lines: if pupils are to take the second language for a public examination in the fifth year it is essential to begin studying it at 13+ (or even at 12+); two years would be inadequate, and therefore, in a sense, offering a second language in the third year is really just pre-dating the customary options procedure by one year in that subject area. But how many pupils in fact complete this three year course? Figures are available for the two case study schools for third year pupils of 1975/76 studying a second language, and those choosing to continue it into the fourth year.

	German		Spanish		Latin	
	3rd yr	4th yr	3rd yr	4th yr	3rd yr	4th yr
West Mercia	90	68	29	68	29	11
Victoria	71	37	–	–	–	6

At Victoria School, where A Band pupils had studied German from the beginning of the second year, 52 per cent chose German as one of their fourth year options. In fact it proved more popular than French, which was chosen by only 34 per cent of the A Band. At West Mercia, where

French remained the first foreign language in the fourth year so that any other language would be an addition not an alternative, the proportion of pupils choosing to continue German (after one year's study) was higher than at Victoria — about 75 per cent. This meant that the projected two sets for fourth year German would be more than filled, and from what he had said earlier in the year the Head of Modern Languages would agree this was satisfactory.

> 'I suppose if you had enough for two sets in the fourth year then I think that would be acceptable. If one set discontinued I think that would be an acceptable wastage, but if they were to come through with only one set . . . I don't think that would be an acceptable wastage.'

But the figures for Spanish and Latin might cause concern, and staff would have to consider whether it was possible to run such small Spanish and Latin sets, or whether it was advisable to try to encourage more pupils to join these classes. So choosing to study a second language in the third year (or earlier) may be rather different in some respects from making choices for the fourth year, which in most schools implies a commitment to the whole of a two year course. If the second language is up for choice again in the fourth year options scheme along with all the other subjects, then the second language experience before the fourth year is in some ways a 'sampling course', where the concept of 'wastage' referred to in the excerpt seems appropriate. Sampling courses may in fact be provided during the third year in other subject areas; for example by ensuring that pupils experience a wide range of craft subjects during the year; but with second language teaching it is usually only a proportion of the year group — those considered linguistically able — who have the opportunity to sample the new subject.

In addition to the issues relating to curriculum planning within the school, wider considerations about the significance of language teaching may play their part in influencing what is offered to pupils. It has already been pointed out that there is a long tradition, in grammar and other selective schools, of beginning a second language in the second or third year and that in many of these schools this was usually for a minority of pupils. This tradition may continue to receive strong support from outside the school, particularly from parents who are concerned that opportunities offered by the grammar school curriculum should not disappear in comprehensive schools. Parental support may encourage schools which had not formerly had a tradition of third year second language courses to provide them, as seems to have been the case at West Mercia School, where there was a strong concern that this new opportunity should be extended to all those incoming pupils who wished to benefit from it.

Whatever the educational merits of offering a second language to the third year, it seems that in many instances it can produce unintended and problematic consequences; questions about who should study one or two languages can become inextricably and emotively bound up with other issues relating to ability. If it is the A Band only who can study German, the argument runs, then German must be a difficult and (therefore) high status subject. Conversely, if a child is studying two languages perhaps this means he is in the 'successful' group of pupils. For the anxious parent new to comprehensive schools, it may seem as if there are ways of ensuring that some pupils are more equal than others.

C. Forms of pupil grouping and the curriculum

It has become fairly clear that in many schools only pupils in certain groups had the option of taking certainn courses in the third year, particularly in foreign languages. This could be equally true of a highly selective school or of one that took the whole ability range. It applied in some measure to both the case study schools. At West Mercia High School, of course, the division of the majority of pupils into W and M bands had been devised in the first place simply to accommodate second language teaching. But even there the arrangement had begun to have other connotations, and in the mind of some was being stretched to fit the more familiar A/B/C band pattern, the H band fitting easily into the C band slot. Victoria Comprehensive provided a good example of this pattern, with clear 'demarcation lines' between the bands; although house groups cut across these lines, during timetabled hours pupils did not mix with those from other bands. And, as we have seen, decisions about which pupils should study foreign languages in the third year were worked out in terms of the band structure. Of course a number of arrangements may be made for grouping pupils by ability for particular subjects, but it is suggested here that one type of organizational decision will influence more profoundly than any other the final shape of the curriculum for this or any other year group; and that is the type of pupil group which is established as the *basic unit* for curriculum planning.

It has already been pointed out in Part II that two-thirds of the original 100 schools organized their pupils in the third year on the basis of ability, although there were many different ways in which this might be done. But many of these schools described their system as 'broad banding' and it is this idea of the Ability Band which needs to be more closely defined here. A band implies a unit containing more than one teaching group, and is only likely to be used in a school with at least a three or four form entry. Furthermore, it usually carries the implication that there is some difference in ability between pupils in the various bands. For the present purpose the term Ability Band will carry this meaning (where a year group is divided into large units according to some criterion other than ability the term block will be used). Figure 3.4 showed that half the twenty schools could be said to organize their third year pupils into bands, according to this definition, but the way in which this structure was used differed from school to school. The third year structure at Victoria would be an example of the Ability Band type, with the Band itself being the main focus of planning, although for much of the timetable the focus could be narrowed to a single class (A1, A2) because there was only a limited amount of regrouping within the band. In other schools, more extensive use was made of the Band as a planning unit, with a variety of groupings being established within it for different subjects. To give a clearer idea of how this might work, there follows a description of the third year organization at two of the eighteen schools with an Ability Band system.

Pinewood School (See Figure 3.5)

Pinewood School is a mixed, 12—16 comprehensive school of about 1200 pupils. Just after the present head arrived,* a grammar school and a secondary modern school had been amalgamated to form the present school which still operates on a split site. The school functioned as a bilateral school until the first comprehensive intake reached the top of the school. It is situated fairly high up, overlooking the town on one side and some country on the other. The intake, according to earlier information, was 'mixed, but mainly working class', the town being 'peculiarly lacking in middle class families resident within its boundaries'. In their last term at middle school pupils took maths, English and reading tests, and were placed in bands when they arrived at the high school, partly on the results of these tests and also as a result of their head teacher's recommendation. For the school year 1975/76, there were two remedial sets in the second year (that is, on entry), compared with one in the third year (3C4). Their work was under the supervision of the remedial department who also serviced other departments.

In this curriculum pattern, there was an extensive amount of regrouping within each band. For English, for example, which was set across each of the A and B Bands, the sets were determined on the basis of a yearly examination and regular classwork which was given marks and grades. There were movements between sets, both termly and yearly; with this proviso, the head of English was happy with the system: 'I think one has to stand up and say "We're academic, we want

---

* He was appointed as head of the grammar school one term before the amalgamation.

Figure 3.5: Pinewood School; third year curriculum pattern 1975/76

Pinewood School   343 pupils in three Ability Bands. 40 period week

Class	No. of pupils	E	M	Langs.	Science	Humanities			
3A1	32	*	*	* L_4	*	$G_3H_3RE_1Mu_2$	$S/S/S_6$	F/F_5	$E/E/E/E_5$
3A2	31	*	*	*	*	$G_3H_3RE_1Mu_2$	PE/PE_2		$C/C/C/C/C_2$
3A3	31	*	*	Sp_4 *	*	$G_3H_3RE_1Mu_2$	$S/S/S_6$	F/F_5	$Ga/Ga/Ga/Ga/Ga_2$
3A4	31	*	*	*	*	$G_3H_3RE_1Mu_2$	PE/PE_2	C/C_4	$M/M/M/M_5$
3B1	31	*	*	*	*	$G_3H_3RE_1Mu_2$	$S/S/S_6$	PE/PE_2	$E/E/E/E_5$
3B2	31	*	*	*	*	$G_3H_3RE_1Mu_2$	F/F_5		$M/M/M/M_5$
3B3	32	*	*	*	*	$G_3H_3RE_1Mu_2$	$S/S/S_6$	PE/PE_2	$C/C/C/C/C_6$
3B4	32	*	*	*	*	$G_3H_3RE_1Mu_2$	F/F_5		$Ga/Ga/Ga/Ga_2$
3C1	28	E_6	M_6		S_4RuSt_2	$SocSt_6RE_2Mu_2$			$C/C/C/C/C_8$
3C2	29	E_6	M_6		S_4RuSt_2	$SocSt_6RE_2Mu_2$			$Ga/Ga/Ga/Ga_2$
3C3	16	E_6	M_6		S_4RuSt_2	$SocSt_6RE_2Mu_2$			
3C4	19	E_6	M_6		S_4RuSt_2	$SocSt_6RE_2Mu_2$			

* means that for this subject pupils are regrouped; these groups appear on the right.

Notes: 1) One p. of H/G/SS to be used for careers as needed.
2) One p. of E to be used for drama if possible.
3) 'Craft' includes technical studies, home studies, commercial studies, art and craft. These may be integrated or alternated according to plans of department.
4) 45–55% of timetable in 'double periods'.

to keep our standards up". I think mixed ability is against this.'
Distinctions between the bands seemed to be fairly explicit and well
understood; the A Band was aiming for O-level, the B Band for CSE,
while non-examination pupils would be in the C Band. The Band
structure could be useful in other ways: there were actually three third
year Parents' Evenings during the year, one for each Band. Although A
and B Band pupils were setted by ability for Maths and French as well
as English, other regroupings within the Band were made on a different
basis. For example, A and B Band Science groups were arranged to
contain approximately 20 pupils, and similar sized groups were formed
in all Bands for craft subjects where a 'rotation of activities' was
followed.

It is fairly easy to point to the *differences* between bands that
appear on the diagram. With regard to the subjects that were common
to all, the A and B Bands had five periods of English and maths, against
six in the C Band, who also had at least two more periods of craft than
anyone else. There were also differences in the subjects studied: pupils
in the C Band did not take French, and had social studies instead of
separately timetabled geography and history. Two of their six periods
of science were devoted to rural studies. The other major difference fell
within, rather than between bands; two of the A Band classes took a
second foreign language, while the subject allocation of the other two
classes was identical to those in the B Band. At the same time, it is
important to point out that within what may appear to be a fairly
traditional structure, revised third year syllabuses had been prepared for
the third year in the following subjects for 1975/76: geography,
history, maths, RE, woodwork and French. In addition, a new course
of integrated science was being developed for the B Band, and one
period of English was to be devoted to drama for all classes. Within the
English department (itself part of a Faculty of Creative Studies) the
staff were working on an 'English across the curriculum' policy. In
other words, it is *not* suggested that the kind of planning unit — the
Ability Band — in every way determines other types of organization in
the school (like the departmental structure, for example), or the
methods used within the classroom. The argument is simply that the
decision to divide the year group into Bands establishes a framework
which may set limits to all subsequent curriculum planning. If, for
instance, the question arises of whether all pupils should take French,
in this situation it is likely to take the form 'Should the C Band take
French?' The headmaster pointed out that in practice there was some
movement between bands — 14 per cent during 1975/76 — but for
most planning purposes, it is the Band which is the primary unit. And,
as the head of English pointed out, a Band in this school is still quite a
large group: 'You need an awful lot of resources when you're teaching

125 children at any one time'. So subject and time allocation, setting arrangements, and to some extent course outlines (for example, 'integrated science') tend to be planned for these large units whose characteristics are well known to experienced teachers even before a set of pupils ('the third year of 75') come to fill them.

The other school to be described has some affinities with Victoria Comprehensive; it is an urban comprehensive with six third year classes. But like Pinewood School this is a 12—16 school, having a total of 700 pupils — only just over half the size of Victoria. With fewer teachers and teaching spaces it might be expected that the timetabling arrangements would need careful tailoring to meet the requirements of the usual sort of third year curriculum. In this situation how would the Ability Band system be used?

Hornbeam School (See Figure 3.6)

Hornbeam School, with a third year group (in 1975/76) of 170 pupils, provides a straightforward example of Ability Bands: three Bands, (A, B and C) each containing two classes, with some differences in curriculum between each Band. In addition to the teaching groups outlined in the curriculum pattern (Figure 3.6), there was a separate house structure for 'registration, welfare, assemblies, competitive games, etc.', and this was not related to ability.

It can be seen from the curriculum pattern (Figure 3.6) that there was a nice balance of different types of grouping and regrouping. The A Band pupils ('the most able, likely to take O-level and some CSE at 16') mixed with other pupils in timetabled hours for games only, but they were regrouped within the Band for several subjects, thus making possible a choice between a second foreign language (German) or more scope on the aesthetic side (art and music); smaller groups for practical subjects; ability sets in French; and regrouping by sex for PE. More complex regroupings were organized for the B and C Bands. Regrouping across the B Band seems to have been arranged primarily for those pupils who were able and willing to continue with French (one group of 20). This amount of time was balanced within the C Band by practical work in small groups, but for most of the time allocated to practical subjects one B class and one C class were combined and pupils given a free choice.[23] It seems that in a school of this size, once the Ability Band structure has provided the outline of the curriculum, it is possible to allow for open choice by individuals within some areas. It is worth noticing that this pattern of choice, added to an Ability Band structure, seemed to be carried through into the fourth year: teaching groups and Band structure remained intact for the compulsory areas of the curriculum (which differed from one Band to another), but options were arranged to straddle the Bands as follows:

Figure 3.6: Hornbeam School; third year curriculum pattern 1975/76.

Hornbeam School   170 pupils in three Ability Bands. 40 period week.

Class	No. of pupils	E	M	Lang. F	Lang. G	Science	Humanities	Regrouped classes	
3A1	31	E_4	M_5	*	*	$B_2Ch_2P_2$	$G_3H_3RE_1Mu_1$	F/F_5 $Ge/Ge/A.Mu._3$ $Wk/Mk/HE_3$ $A/TD/Nk_3$ PE/PE_1	
3A2	31	E_4	M_5	*	*	$B_2Ch_2P_2$	$G_3H_3RE_1Mu_1$		
3B1	29	E_5	M_5	*		$B_2Ch_2P_2$	$G_3H_3RE_2Mu_2$	$F/TD/Nk_2$ $F/Wk/Mk_3$ $F/Lb/Lb_1$	$A/Mk/Nk_2$ $Wk/TD/HE_3$ (3B1, C1) PE/PE_1
3B2	28	E_5	M_5	*		$B_2Ch_2P_2$	$G_3H_3RE_2Mu_2$		$A/Mk/Wk_2$ $Wk/TD/HE_3$ (3B2, C2) PE/PE_1
3C1	24	E_6	M_5			$B_2Ch_2P_2$	$G_3H_3RE_2Mu_2$	$A/Wk/Mk_2$ $A/A/HE_2$	
3C2	27	E_6	M_5			$B_2Ch_2P_2$	$G_3H_3RE_2Mu_2$		

Far-right regrouped groups (with brace):

$Ga/Ga/Ga/Ga$ (3A1, 3B1, 3C1)
$Ga/Ga/Ga/Ga_2$ (3A2, 3B2, 3C2)

* means that for this subject pupils are regrouped; these groups appear on the right.

Notes:
1) Pupils from B1 and B2 who take French have F_5
2) Numbers of boys and girls for all regrouped classes given; for example, see page 115.
3) 45—50% of timetable in 'double periods'.

Band A	1 subject from Option I	(3 subjects)	
	1 subject from Option II	(9 subjects)	
	1 subject from Option III	(7 subjects)	Band B
	1 subject from Option IV	(6 subjects)	
Band C	1 subject from Group 1	(2 subjects)	
	1 subject from Group 2	(3 subjects)	
	1 subject from Group 3	(3 subjects)	
	1 subject from Group 4	(3 subjects)	

Several reasons may lie behind the decision to adopt the Band as the unit of organization. From a limited practical point of view, it may simply represent one way of getting away from the 'jigsaw' approach to timetabling, where the planner is obliged to juggle with a very large number of single class/teacher units; at least with Ability Bands one can consider the needs of a sizeable proportion of a year group at one time. But there are likely to be a number of other, more fundamental, considerations, all connected with the view that to group the pupils (however broadly) according to ability is in their best interests, as well as representing the most economic use of specialist resources. For example, this teacher, while confessing to a certain ambivalence, has few doubts that this is the most useful approach:

'I suppose it's differentiating between pupils, which perhaps we shouldn't do, but to some extent if you're eventually going to think about exams you've got to think in terms of some of them being eight or nine subject pupils, and others being only five or six subject pupils . . . You could argue that I'd be splitting it up into a sort of grammar school and secondary modern elements, but I'd like to feel that one can go for three genuine bands where the options offered in each of the three bands are slightly different.' (West Mercia)

The Ability Band structure, it can be argued, makes it possible to adapt the third year curriculum to suit the needs of broadly defined groups of pupils. This may involve some differences in the subjects studied. More generally, because each Band contains only part of the whole ability range, teachers can adapt the content of the course and the classroom methods to the needs of the Band — while recognizing that there might still be a considerable spread of ability within one class. The significance of adopting the Ability Band as a planning unit is that while the planning task is simplified (especially if all classes within the Band are treated identically, either in basic teaching groups or open sets across the Band), decisions about what is best for certain ability groups become to some extent embedded in the timetable structure. But it must be stressed that there are many variations on the pattern, some much more flexible than others.

With a year group of more than about three or four classes it is often necessary to break it into smaller units of some kind for timetabling purposes. But there are other criteria than ability which could be used. For example, a mixed year group could be split into two halves — boys and girls. Where two single sex schools have been amalgamated this has sometimes been the case during a transition period, but it is against the spirit of the times and one cannot imagine that idea being widely adopted. The other obvious approach is to establish a number of units, probably of roughly equal size, each of which is a microcosm of the whole year group. These units could be related to some other structure — a house system, for example. I have called this sort of unit a *Block*. This term is used to show that a decision has been made that these groupings exist purely for administrative convenience and do not relate to ability or aptitude; the corollary is that an identical curriculum pattern is drawn up for each Block. In planning terms this represents a further move towards simplicity: in effect the designer has only to plan for one quarter (or whatever) of the year group, and if premises and staffing permit, the timetable itself can be replicated for each of the Blocks. As with the Ability Band, the question of pupil grouping within the Block is left open. They may be kept in their basic teaching groups, or regrouped for some or all subjects. The question of regrouping may be left for each department to work out for itself. The important consequence of this approach, especially in a large school, is that while reducing the planning task to manageable proportions it leaves a very large number of options open for decision at a later stage of the planning process, and possibly by different groups within the staff team. The only fixed point is that each Block is a cross section of the year group in terms of ability.

Only two of the eighteen schools had adopted this form of organization for their third year group. Both were large well-established 11—18 comprehensive schools, and both had developed their present curriculum structure after lengthy experience of other forms of organization, including Ability Banding or streaming. The Block systems outlined below had been introduced within the last five years.

At Lime School, there were four Blocks, each attached to a House and containing three classes in which pupils spent at least 22 of the 40 periods. But for some purposes two Blocks were combined into a single unit for regrouping. At Sycamore School, on the other hand, the emphasis was on flexibility within a common structure; within each self-contained Block of three classes,* for which, as at Lime School,

---

*   In fact three of the four Blocks had three classes; the other Block only had two.

Figure 3.7: Sycamore School; third year curriculum pattern 1975/76

Sycamore School   334 pupils in four blocks; 3 of 3 classes, 1 of 2 classes. 40 period week

Class	No. of pupils	E	M	Lang.	Science	Humanities				
						G_2	H_2	RE_2	Mu_2	$HE/HE/HE/HE_4$
3.1	26 + 6	E_4	*	**	***	G_2	H_2	RE_2	Mu_2	$S/S/S_6$
3.2	27 + 4	E_4				G_2	H_2	RE_2	Mu_2	$M/M/M/M_4$
3.3	26 + 5	E_4				G_2	H_2	RE_2	Mu_2	$Lan/Lan/Lan/Lan/Lan_6$
		E_4								$A.C/A.C/A.C/A.C_4$

This pattern is repeated for the other three class blocks. The two-class block, with no remedial pupils is given below:

3.4	28	E_4	*	**	***	G_2	H_2	RE_2	Mu_2	$HE/HE/HE_4$
										$S/S/S_6$
3.5	27	E_4				G_2	H_2	RE_2	Mu_2	$M/M/M_4$
										$A.C/A.C/A.C_4$
										$Lan/Lan/Lan_6$

* means that for this subject pupils are regrouped; these groups appear on the right.

Notes:
1) There are generally four teachers to a 3 class block. For English and the humanities, the 'extra' teacher usually takes a remedial group composed of some pupils from each class.
2) Lan = Languages; this includes French, German and classical studies and is set by ability. The programme varies, e.g. Set 1: $F4G_2$. Set 2: F_6. Set 3: F_2 Cl.St.4. Set 4: Cl.St.6. Maths is also set by ability.
3) Science, home economics and art/craft are taught in mixed ability small groups. Science is divided into biology/chemistry, chemistry/physics, and physics/biology on the timetable.
4) 100% of the timetable is in 'double periods'.

there was a common timetable, many departments were encouraged to adopt whatever form of grouping they found most useful for their subject, given that four staff members were allocated to a Block.

Sycamore School (See Figure 3.7)

Sycamore School is a girls' comprehensive school of about 1400 pupils. It has grown steadily in size over the last ten years, absorbing another school in the process. Until recently its intake was 'creamed' by two nearby grammar schools; these are now receiving a non-selective intake. In 1974 the intake was described as 'almost wholly working class'. The Headmistress commented then: 'This school is only just beginning to get off the ground. It is bubbling with ideas that are beginning to develop well, but there is not a lot to be seen yet.' There were in fact eleven tutor groups in the third year of 1975/76. Three Blocks each contained three classes made up, as indicated in the diagram, of a basic group of about 27 and a small remedial group. In the fourth Block there were only two classes and no remedial pupils. The common timetable structure of the Block was used in different ways for different subjects. In English and the three humanities subjects, one teacher taught each basic group and a fourth took a remedial group composed of all the pupils designated as remedial within the Block. For maths the whole Block was divided into four ability sets. For home economics, science and art/craft, there were again four groups but these were mixed ability groups. The inherent simplicity of the timetable was enhanced by the fact that for the third year the nominally 40 period week was all taught in double units of 70 minutes. The only explicit differentiation in the curriculum outline was within the six periods allotted to language. However, the use of this Block system in no way imposed uniformity within each Block; maths sets, for instance, could be following separate syllabuses or proceeding at a very different pace, while the identical timetable for each Block of three classes opened up possibilities for team teaching (employed in English) and variable sizes of group.

Lime School (See Figure 3.8)

The Block system at Lime School enlarged the area of differentiation slightly by placing languages other than English outside the common Block pattern and grouping them with craft subjects in the open sets that ran across two Blocks. This arrangement should be seen within the context of the school's background. It is an 11–18 urban comprehensive school designated as a future 'Community College' in an Educational Priority Area, taking a considerable number of pupils for whom English is not their first language; in this context, there may be different priorities in language teaching. What is more interesting than

Figure 3.8: Lime School; third year curriculum pattern 1975/76

Lime School 360 pupils in four house blocks. 40 period week.

Class	No. of pupils	E	M	Langs.	Science	Humanities					
3E1	30	E_5	M_5		S_4	G_2	H_3	RE_2	TP_1	$A/A/A/A_2$	$PE/PE/PE/PE/PE/PE_2$
3E2	30	E_5	M_5		S_4	G_2	H_3	RE_2	TP_1	$Mu/Mu/Mu/Mu_2$	$TD/TD/TD/Nk/Nk/Nk_2$
3E2	30	E_5	M_5		S_4	G_2	H_3	RE_2	TP_1		$F/PE/PE/PE_2$
											$Ger/F/C/C/C/C_4$
											$C/C/C/C/HE/HE/HE/$
											HE/HE_4
3W1	30	E_5	M_5		S_4	G_2	H_3	RE_2	TP_1	$A/A/A/A_2$	
3W2	30	E_5	M_5		S_4	G_2	H_3	RE_2	TP_1	$Mu/Mu/Mu/Mu_2$	
3W3	30	E_5	M_5		S_4	G_2	H_3	RE_2	TP_1		

Notes:

1) This pattern was repeated for the other half of the year group, in 3N and 3S

2) Where class groups are bracketed together, eg. $\left(\begin{array}{c} E_5 \\ E_5 \\ E_5 \end{array} \right.$ this indicates that they have a common timetable.

3) TP = Tutor period

4) 90% of the timetable was in 'double periods'.

this deviation from a common course is the way in which the Block system has been developed to express the basic educational design of the school. Before 1972 the school had a purely vertical house structure and a smaller population. When the school increased to twelve form entry by absorbing another local school this structure became impracticable. This led to a complete re-thinking of the school's organization, which now included a lower school (first and second years) and a middle school (third and fourth years), each divided into four houses. To quote the school's own handbook:

> 'There seemed little point in retaining a social structure which was not completely meaningful and realistic *all* day, every day. A social structure in which pupils meet for registration, at lunchtime, and for an odd house period necessarily must be infinitely less effective than one in which the social unit is meaningful and realistic throughout the day, i.e. one in which the *social* unit is *also* the *learning* unit.'

This design, then, found its expression in the four Blocks (houses) each with their three classes (tutor groups). Since these tutor groups were quite explicitly mixed ability groups, it might be thought that this left little room for providing pupils with a curriculum adapted to their particular ability and aptitude; was this not imposing an unwarranted degree of uniformity in a misguided drive for 'equality'? The answer of the staff would be that the needs of the pupils are best met at an *individual* level, and this can be done just as effectively within the unstreamed basic teaching group as by any system of ability grouping, which can never produce entirely homogeneous units.

Here, then, the Block system was being used to implement a specific and carefully thought out educational design; but the important characteristic of this approach is that by simplifying the timetable structure it enables those responsible for planning the curriculum to consider the implications of alternate forms of organization, all of which may be possible within the framework, before deciding which is desirable and for what purpose; equally, changes can be made within the Block without disturbing any other classes or year groups.[24]

So far we have looked at units of organization that would be appropriate for large schools. Nothing much has been said about the most familiar unit of organization to be found in schools of all sizes, the class, or *form* as it has been known for so long. Traditionally this was a group of pupils, from 20 to 40 or more in number, presided over by a form master or mistress and based in a formroom, in which they might receive many of their lessons, possibly from the same form teacher. In any case they would be taught as a single group for much of the week.

In other words, this was the sort of arrangement described in Part I, originating in the grammar schools, and becoming common in all kinds of secondary school after 1945. But the word 'form' has lost its shape, as it has been stretched to cover a number of different arrangements in schools. So for the present purposes we shall substitute the term coined by Davies (1969): 'primary group': a group of thirty or so pupils who are treated as a single unit for pastoral and teaching purposes. The 'pure' variety of this would be when the pupils were never regrouped for any subject and their timetable was constructed in such a way that it did not overlap with that of any other form. Each Primary Group might be following the same course outline, or their programmes might vary widely. There was at least one example of this arrangement among the eighteen schools: this was at Elm School, a girls' grammar school, where the three parallel classes followed an identical course but remained in their Primary Groups all the week.

More commonly, the Primary Group has been 'downgraded' as Davies puts it; the group does not remain intact for the whole week but its pupils are regrouped or setted for some subjects. If regrouping takes place for more than one or two subjects, it is likely that the focus for planning will shift to the large group of which the form is a part. On the other hand, in a small school the focus may move to sub-groups within the form; in a one form entry school this sub-dividing may be the only way of providing the 'minority' subjects, as for example at Maple School:

E_5 M/M_4 S_4 G_3 H_3 PE_3 Ga_2 $F/RE.RSc_4$ Ge/A_3 $Orch/MArith_1$ Wk/HE_4 Mk/Nk_2 $TD/HuBi_2$

A type of covert Primary Group is found where pupils who constitute an easily recognizable *teaching* group for most of the week belong to totally different *pastoral* units, which are their 'official' identity groups, each with its tutor, but which seldom or never meet for lessons. The main difference here is that no one teacher is responsible for the teaching group in the way that a form master or mistress would be. It is likely that in these cases another type of unit is the main focus of curriculum planning, and this was so at both Victoria and West Mercia Schools.

It has been implied that this traditional pupil unit — the Primary Group — is most likely to be found in schools of a 'traditional' size; schools with a two or three form entry. But it is equally possible for a school of modest size to treat the entire year group, or a large part of it, as a single unit for planning purposes, and this seems to have been the case at Rowan School, an 11–16 comprehensive school where three of the four classes spent only eight of the forty periods in their Primary

Groups, and were regrouped in a variety of ways for the rest of the time. So if a school has decided to keep the third year in Primary Groups, so that these become the main planning units for curriculum and timetabling purposes, this probably reflects the wider aims of the school. Thus it is likely that the school places a strong emphasis on the stability of the Primary Group and the benefits this brings, valuing this more highly than regrouping by specific ability for the different subjects, or the departmental autonomy that could follow from 'blocking' the timetable to permit a variety of groupings — as would be possible with Blocks or Ability Bands. Of course it is possible to combine the systems, and have Primary Groups within Blocks or Bands, as was the case at Lime School. So large schools may make use of Primary Groups, probably within some larger unit. Indeed, 'fine streaming' based on Primary Groups was until recently widely considered to be one of the best ways of combining group stability with efficient teaching in large schools. It should be clear from the timetable and the general aims of the school whether it is the Primary Group or some larger unit that is the main focus of planning.

This difference of approach can be brought out by comparing the pattern of West Mercia with that of another large comprehensive, Redwood School. It has been explained that pupils at West Mercia spent some time together in their teaching groups (3W1, 3M2), and for an individual teacher this might be the grouping that mattered because it was the class unit that he regularly taught. But for a visitor in the school it was sometimes difficult to communicate with any one teaching group just because there was no teacher responsible for it, and it therefore had no existence in an administrative sense. And since these teaching groups were parallel in ability, it made sense to deal with them in larger units for curriculum planning. Only in the later stages of the timetabling process was it necessary to deal with teaching groups as single units which could be fitted into those parts of the timetable which were not blocked across the band. So references in the staffroom tended to be either to the tutor group (for pastoral matters) or, for lesson planning purposes, to the band; for instance, was some new idea or book appropriate for the W band, or would a television programme be more helpful for the H band than for the rest of the year group?

At Redwood School, which had much more explicitly defined Ability Bands, Primary Groups were considered very important by the staff. The school is in an Educational Priority Area, a context in which pastoral issues common to all schools often stand out more sharply. So although the Band structure was clearly related to public examination prospects:

'Broadly speaking, pupils in 3A . . . all go forward to a full GCE

O-level course, pupils in 3B ... begin courses leading to CSE
Mode I examinations and those in 3C follow courses leading
mainly to CSE Mode 3 examinations.'

the real concerns for this year group were seen to lie elsewhere:

'The third year is essentially one of diagnosis and guidance. To
this end emphasis is laid by the Head of Year on strong
tutor/pupil links and a careers information programme ... Two
hours out of 25 one-hour periods each week are devoted to
pastoral periods where each tutor arranges the activity for his or
her group in order to build up a close pastoral relationship.'

This conscious fostering of a Primary Group atmosphere, combined
with the fact that over two-thirds of the week was spent in these groups
by all pupils, indicates again that it is possible to focus attention on the
smaller unit even in a large school or year group.

Ash School (See Figure 3.9)

There was one other comprehensive school among the eighteen
where pupils spent nearly all their time in Primary Groups and the
timetable seemed to be planned around these. This also makes an
interesting comparison with West Mercia High, in this case because it is
another 13—18 high school: Ash School, with a seven form entry,
drawn from two middle schools. The seven teaching groups in which
pupils were placed on entry were also their pastoral and social units,
since the school was organized on a year-group basis rather than a house
system. When the pupils were in their last year at the middle schools,
their parents were asked to choose between a second language or a
practical bias for their children. This recommendation, together with
records from middle schools, was used to place pupils in forms. So
while the general pattern of the third year course could be seen as
similar for all groups, the differences within it were tailored to suit
parental choice in the case of the second language/practical bias, and
pupils' abilities in the case of individual or general sciences. This can be
seen in detail on the curriculum pattern for the school (Figure 3.9), and
this is how the arrangement was described by the school:

3S	3K	3Y	Parallel forms setted for Maths. Of these 3S and 3K will take two foreign languages.
3B	3L		Pupils taking French and a course with a practical bias. The better mathematicians will be in 3B and this form will also take individual sciences. 3L will take General Science.
	3U	3E	Pupils taking no foreign language.

Figure 3.9: Ash School; third year curriculum pattern 1975/76

Ash School 206 pupils in three graded Ability Bands. 40 period week.

Class	No. of pupils	E	M	Lang.	Science	Humanities			
3S	30	E_5	*	F_5Ge_5	$B_2Ch_2P_2$	$G_2H_2RE_1Mu_1$	A_2 Mk/Nk$_2$	} Ga/Ga4	} M/M/M$_5$
3K	33	E_5	*	F_5Ge_5	$B_2Ch_2P_2$	$G_2H_2RE_1Mu_1$	A_2 Mk/Nk$_2$		
3Y	33	E_6	*	F_5	$B_2Ch_2P_2$	$G_2H_2RE_1Mu_1$	A_2 TD/Nk$_2$	} Ga/Ga4	
3B	28	E_6	5	F_5	$B_2Ch_2P_2$	$G_2H_2RE_1Mu_1$	A_2 TD/Nk$_2$	} Wk/Wk/HE/HE/HE4	
3L	30	E_7	5	F_5	Gen Sc.4	$G_2H_2RE_1Mu_2$	A_2 TD/Nk$_2$	HE/Wk4	
3U	28	E_7	6		Gen Sc.4	$G_2H_2RE_2Mu_2$	A_2 RS/Nk$_3$	HE/C4LC2	} Ga/Ga4
3E	24	E_7	6		Gen Sc.4	$G_2H_2RE_2Mu_2$	A_2 RS/Nk$_3$	HE/C4LC2Ga4 (with 3Y and 3B)	

* means that for this subject pupils are regrouped; these groups appear on the right.

Notes: 1) RS = Rural Studies, LC = Light Craft.
2) 75—90% of the timetable in 'double periods'.

So at this school, where pupils were offered much the same sort of choice within the curriculum as at West Mercia, it had been found feasible to establish stable Primary Groups on the basis of both parental choice and the needs of the pupils as assessed by the school. In a 13+ high school, stability is clearly important; there is only one year for staff and pupils to get to know each other before the beginning of fourth year examination-orientated courses, and membership of a stable Primary Group may well help pupils to settle down quickly within their new school. These suggestions are strengthened by the rather similar system at the eleven form entry 13+ high school, Oak School, where much of the timetable was arranged on a Primary Group basis (within Ability Bands).

This review of the more widely used methods for structuring third year groups for teaching suggests some thoughts about how the form of grouping can influence the curriculum at the initial or central planning stage, when the head sits down with the senior staff team to review the general school policy. Of course, they will be concerned with all the years in the school, and our preoccupation with the third year may well have led us to neglect some factors that affect the school as a whole, especially in the eighteen schools.[25] (It was because we wished to see the third year in the context of the whole school that we concentrated so much of our time in Stage Two of the Study on the two case study schools.) But the particular concerns of the third year — pressure for some differentiation and concern to maintain a balanced curriculum — may reveal more clearly than with most other years where the school's priorities are. For example, where a school decides on Ability Banding, it follows that the planners consider that grouping by ability, however broadly that is interpreted, is so important that it should be built into the curriculum structure at this initial stage. A decision to focus on Primary Groups, on the other hand, would leave several questions open: for example whether groups should be parallel or graded in ability and whether or not all groups should follow the same course. But the implication of this decision is that pupils will gain more from being in a stable group than from any attempts to meet individual differences by extensive use of setting or other types of regrouping. Indeed it could be argued in defence of mixed ability Primary Groups that since no one group of pupils is truly homogeneous it is more profitable to recognize this explicitly by providing for individual differences *within* a clearly heterogeneous group. But if, as seems widely accepted, pupils in the third year are to be given the opportunity to diverge, if only slightly, from a common course outline, either Primary Groups must be combined and regrouped to allow pupils to follow minority courses, or pupils must be allotted to Primary Groups on the basis of these differences — a second language class, for example. Once again this means that decisions about the detailed working of the curriculum have to be written in by the central planning team. The Block approach sets fewer limits at the central planning stage, although it may stretch the resources of staffing and accommodation. Not only is the timetabling task simplified, but decisions about grouping and the detailed allocation of subject time can be left until a later stage, when the characteristics of the year group may be better known and any changes in the staff team can be taken into account. One other important argument for this approach was put forward by one of the senior staff at Sycamore School, in commenting on the draft description of their Block system for the third year:

'The value of this approach is that it allows staff to acquire expertise in planning which they are going to need if we are to produce adequate educational management in the future. By allowing them room to be good it also allows them room to be indifferent or even bad, but this can be dealt with in other ways than keeping all decisions at the centre.'

3. Devolution in curriculum planning: the use of time

This concept of devolution in curriculum planning can be applied to other areas besides pupil grouping. One of these is the organization of time within the school day. While we were in the case study schools we spent some time early in the year with single classes, joining them for a day at a time and going round the school with them to all their lessons. The most immediate experience, to us as adults, was one of fragmented time — up to eight different lessons, in different parts of the school, quite apart from assemblies, meals and other breaks. Of course there were exceptions — two, or even three, periods spent in the workshops, laboratories or the art room — and many pupils said they liked the variety, but the experience did draw one's attention to this aspect of timetabling. There seem to be two issues, which are related. In the first place, who decides how each period is spent, and secondly, into what size of unit is the school day to be divided? One set of answers to these questions leads to the jigsaw model of the timetable, a painstaking compilation of many small pieces, which should leave no one in doubt about where he should be at any given time. Because of its complexity it must all be compiled centrally, under one person's direction, taking into consideration the special requirements of all departments.

Another set of answers can result in a modular or open plan timetable, where fairly large units — possibly of groups of pupils or subjects, but probably also of time — are outlined on the timetable, the details to be filled in later by other groups of teachers. As usual, few real third year timetables that we looked at conformed neatly to such models. At West Mercia, for example, time for practical subjects was arranged in this modular way; units of seventy minutes or more were blocked across five or ten classes, a group of up to twelve teachers was listed and the disposition of pupils within this time was left to the teachers concerned. Subjects which were set by ability, like maths and modern languages, also had some leeway on the timetable, but for most of the third year timetable the pattern of teachers and classes interlocked with the pattern for other year groups, so that it resembled more nearly the jigsaw model. This was also the case at Victoria Comprehensive School where, it will be remembered, the struggle to find time for all the subjects had led to a move away from a 35 period week to a 40 period week. Indeed, if the length of the basic time unit is increased — as had happened in practice at five comprehensive schools[26] — either the individual subjects have to be grouped or integrated in some way, or the timetable cycle itself has to be extended, as had been done at Hazel School where there were forty lesson units, each of seventy minutes, in a ten-day cycle.

The Newsom Report spoke of the 'different rhythm of work which is appropriate for different subjects'[27], while considering that by the age of fourteen most of the pupils were able to concentrate for longer than an hour and a half 'when the nature of the work makes this natural'. In the light of some third year timetables, even an hour and a half may be considered a large unit. But the way in which units of time are regarded may be much more important than their absolute length. Spans of time which may appear long on the timetable can be broken down into much smaller units of different types of activity at the classroom level, as they might be in the primary class or at an adults' day conference. These decisions about how a span of time should be broken up — the activities to be pursued, the size and type of group appropriate to these activities, the sort of supervision that is required — can be taken at departmental level, as long as the centrally devised plan provides the framework; what is more, the plan can be changed fairly easily without disturbing that framework in any way.

In fact this sort of departmental planning may be common practice in certain departments; for instance, for PE and games a large group of pupils, possibly of mixed (academic) ability, may be allocated to a team of teachers. It is then up to the teachers concerned to divide the total group into sub-groups according to the activities they want to teach during the allotted time. In this case, the influence of other factors — the season, the weather, the facilities available (is the sports hall needed for public examinations or special competitions?) — makes a flexible approach essential, and this is not considered remarkable. Moreover, in this area of the curriculum it is often accepted that pupils will spend varying amounts of time on the activities provided, and that what is laid down on the timetable should be seen as a minimum requirement. Thus, extra practices for school teams or individuals as well as voluntary lunch-hour clubs and Saturday matches are seen as hovering on the borderline between 'curricular' and 'extracurricular' activities. A similar outlook may prevail in the aesthetic/practical area, where time is almost always allotted in units of at least 60 or 70 minutes and, quite often, longer — perhaps a whole afternoon or morning. Of course this time may then be broken up into conventional, monotechnic units — one group, with one teacher, following through one activity for one (long) session in one place. But a group of teachers with a fairly large group of pupils and perhaps several work areas may be free to use these resources of space and time in a variety of ways.

What may be fairly common practice in the 'non-classroom' subjects may seem less desirable or convenient for the rest of the curriculum. For a start, what length of unit is appropriate for each subject — or each class? It is often argued that some types of learning are best absorbed on a drip-feed principle, in small daily doses. Thus modern languages learning may demand regular short practice sessions and maths may flourish in a similar regime. In fact, it was the problem of reconciling the different sorts of time required by the language and practical areas that led the timetable planners at West Mercia to group third year 'second language' and 'practical' pupils into two bands with different timetable rhythms. But arguments have also been made for a totally different approach to language teaching; for instance, the provision of intensive courses lasting a week or so where the language is used all day in a variety of situations. In the third year, science is commonly allocated a number of double periods, on the assumption that it is a 'practical' subject and units of this length are needed for experimental work. But if the work in hand is of a more theoretical nature, 80 minutes can be a long time to sit on a laboratory stool. For English and the humanities subjects, attitudes to time seem less clear-cut; a single period of 35/40 minutes may be too short for work involving the use of resource materials, but on the other hand if the two periods allotted, say, to history in the third year are allocated as a single unit of 80 minutes, teachers may feel that this makes the whole subject too vulnerable to the vagaries of half term, open days or other occasional events. And what about the other sorts of activities that teachers of these subjects might wish to undertake? If the period length is short and is part of a highly structured school day, how feasible is it for teachers to take pupils out of the classroom, let alone out of the school? Any such diversion from 'desk work', however integral to the curricular programme, may need advanced planning of a high order, involving a number of teachers in other subject areas. It is not altogether surprising that it is in June and July, when during and after public examinations the normal routine has to give way to special orders posted on the staffroom noticeboard, that there is a sudden flurry of history and geography expeditions for the lower part of the school. While the limitations on such expeditions outside the school may be primarily related to financial and logistic considerations rather than to the timetable, more modest activities outside the classroom but on the school premises, can be difficult to arrange within a timetable structure based on small units of time.

It is understandable that attitudes to the use of time may vary from subject to subject, and from school to school. But perhaps some of the everyday timetabling problems — periods too short, too long, unfairly distributed through the week, unrelated to the geographical realities of the school — are exacerbated by the underlying conception of how time has to be structured in the secondary school. Walton (1973)[28] suggests that the basic problem in this situation is that no allowance is made for 'slack', that is time which is not tightly programmed. The concept of 'slack' was borrowed by Shaw (1972)[29] from industry, where it could be defined as surplus productive capacity which could be mobilised to meet sudden fluctuations. In education 'slack' could be seen as time that is not highly programmed. 'Slack does not mean idle or waiting time; it is simply not programmed in advance'. Shaw suggested that in educational settings other than the secondary school there is generally a more flexible outlook. In the early years of the primary school, slack might consist of expressive and semi-recreational activity amounting to perhaps 20 per cent of the time. In higher education, slack might consist of free periods, library, private study or laboratory time to be used by the student at his own discretion.

The secondary school on the other hand, 'programmes all the time for all the pupils'. Why is this? Walton considers that it may be the result of several pressures: the dominance of the curriculum by public examinations, the increase in the number of secondary school subjects, and the tension between vocational demands and the attempt to give a general education. These could all be related to the problems presented by mass formal state education, and the apparent necessity for schools to deliver an agreed 'package' within a limited period of compulsory schooling: 'a lot of children have to be taught, as economically as possible, that knowledge which society consideres to be desirable'.[30]

More pragmatic considerations might be put forward within the schools. Any organization providing a variety of activities for some hundreds of individuals within a limited space and time has to be well structured if productive work is to be carried on and anarchy avoided. But perhaps this need for sound planning has become caught up too closely with the detailed specification of the curriculum. If the tendency is more pronounced within secondary schools, it may be most obvious at the third year level. Thus for the pupils in the first two years — 11—13 — the timetable may look more 'open' because of planning decisions about the needs of children at this age; perhaps pupils should spend blocks of time with one or more teachers in a 'home base' to ease the transition from primary school, or the work time may be divided between large integrated subject areas. Again, even with the pressure of public examinations, it may be possible to sketch out much of the timetable for the fourth and fifth year pupils in terms of 'option blocks' occupying equal amounts of time, and for the sixth form a more flexible approach to time is often considered an appropriate way of encouraging a more mature response from students. But for the third year, the planners in a comprehensive school may have to take into account two pressures that tend to fragment the time. In the first place there are pressures to include a large number of individual subjects, as we have already seen. Secondly, faced with this array of subjects, teachers and parents may well consider that it may be appropriate for pupils of 13—14 to follow slightly different paths according to their ability and interest. In the effort to meet these requirements the timetable planner may find himself back to struggling with the jigsaw, and any idea of building 'slack' into the whole picture seems irrelevant if not laughable.

Is there any way out of this problem? As long as certain conditions have to be met — specified numbers of pupils and staff to be occupied on the premises within specified hours — then in one sense those in charge of the school have to programme all the time for all the pupils. That is, everyone has to follow an agreed schedule. But if, as I suggested earlier, the 'master schedule', the timetable for the whole school, is laid down in outline terms initially, then the 'slack' can be built into the programme as the details are worked out at various levels — by department, by teams of teachers, by teacher and pupils within the classroom. In the crowded third year timetable of many schools at present, slack of a sort may be introduced into the day despite rather than within the system, in a number of ways with which teachers and pupils are only too familiar; dawdling between classrooms; finishing a cup of coffee after the bell has gone; 'tidying up' or 'putting away' and innumerable other 'coping strategies'; but all this is recognized to be a misinterpretation or even a direct contravention of the official programme laid down in the timetable, and usually provokes recurrent waves of 'tightening up'. With a more flexible approach, where many teachers (and perhaps the pupils themselves) are involved in planning how time should be used, it may be easier to provide for the varying curricular needs of groups of individuals, and to replace the frenzy of the inter-lesson 'all change' with a more varied rhythm of work within the larger time blocks. In the third year context, it may only be the remedial teachers at some schools who are given this degree of control over their timetable.

Once again, the key to a more flexible approach to the use of time of this (or any) year group seems to lie in devolution — devolution in the detailed working out of the timetable. The analysis of third year timetables in the twenty schools brought out the tendency of many larger schools to use longer time units for much of the week. If these longer 'periods' are still allocated from the centre to individual teacher/class units, then the problem remains the conventional one writ slightly larger; how the individual teacher structures time in his own subject with his 'own' class. But if groups of teachers are encouraged to plan these, or even longer units, together, then they may produce new solutions to the problems of providing for all the needs of all the pupils.

Notes

1. But the changes in pastoral organization were arrived at after a number of consultations, and formal discussions of some aspects of school policy, including curriculum, became more common.
2. The diagnostic first term was instituted in September 1976. At the end of that term, departments were free to continue as they thought best: with mixed ability teaching; by setting; or by banding. It was hoped that eventually mixed ability teaching would be the norm for the first year, with a blocking system to allow for setting within the blocks for academic subjects in years two and three.
3. For a detailed study of options in the two schools, see Hurman, *A Charter for Choice*, (in press).
4. The aim was to offer as many subjects as possible at three levels: O-level, CSE, and 'school assessed', i.e. leading to an internal rather than an external examination.
5. See page 56 for a full description.
6. We have called the bands W(est), M(ercia) and H(igh) to indicate that they were not intended to follow the conventional A, B, C pattern. What was the reality behind the assumption that, after 1972, the W band were 'more able' than the M band? Comparisons of this sort are notoriously difficult, and since there was no general policy of screening the whole year group on entry it is difficult to settle on a valid criterion. But in 1975 all pupils *were* tested in maths and French before setting was carried out; this showed that there was a considerable overlap between the lowest W band set and the top M band set in both subjects, but on balance the W band were potentially more able. At the end of the year, common examinations were set for both bands in most subjects, and again the English results showed that while large numbers of pupils in both bands lay towards the middle of the distribution curve, the average mark for the W band (about 49 per cent) was higher than that for the M band (about 38 per cent); a clear but not a vast differential. There was a similar pattern in the science results.
7. A more detailed account of these plans and how they were arrived at is given in the case studies of the two schools to appear in this series.

8. For details of how the eighteen schools were selected see Appendix A.

9. Many schools have a system of houses and tutor groups, but these are usually or primarily for pastoral or other non-teaching purposes. The groupings mentioned here are those adopted for timetabled activities.

10. Riesman, D., Gusfield, J. and Gamson, Z., *Academic Values and Mass Education*, N.Y., Doubleday, (1970) p. 10.

11. Westbury, Ian. 'Conventional Classrooms, "Open" Classrooms and the Technology of Teaching,' *Journal of Curriculum Studies*, 5, No. 2, 1973, p. 99.

12. Walker, Decker F. 'What Curriculum Research?', *Journal of Curriculum Studies*, 5, No. 1, 1973, p. 58.

13. See Davies (1969), p. 68; the curriculum unit or 'notional class' is there set at one-ninth of the week, partly because he found this to be a common pattern in many schools where each pupil joined nine 'classes' per week. It provides a useful common unit for comparing timetables which use different units of measurement.

14. But some of the teachers at West Mercia were not satisfied about this and thought that the H band — the slower learners — should spend more time on these basic subjects and less, for example on Science where there was also a common allocation of 7 periods for all third year pupils, in 1975/76.

15. In this case we know that the common timetable outlined was complemented by a common syllabus in history, geography and RE respectively, and (for eighty per cent of the pupils) a common examination in the summer term.

16. At one school which was involved in an earlier part of the study, pupils followed an integrated humanities programme up to the end of the third year. When they came to make choices for the fourth year some of them were confused by subject names which they had not met before, in the school, and wanted to know what 'geography' and 'history' would be about.

17. Another forthcoming study in this series is directly concerned with third year science in the eighteen background schools.

18. Newsom Report, (1963), p. 124.

19. *Man, A Course of Study* (MACOS), (1968), Curriculum Development Associates, Inc., Washington, DC/Centre for Applied Research in Education, University of East Anglia, Norwich.

20. See p. 82.

21. See pp. 135—136.

22. The deputy headmistress of Sycamore School commented:

> 'The provision of two foreign languages can create problems in most comprehensive schools, and any solution to these problems will have limitations'.

23. The result of this choice are given on page 115.

24. The Headmaster of Hazel School (which had twelve classes in ability bands with a common course outline for all but two classes) told us that a change was planned for the third year in 1976/77:

> 'We have now gone beyond the previous position and have blocked the third year in three groups of 4 classes — one A band class, with three B band classes in two groups, also with the remedial and the semi-remedial. Within the blocking it is now possible for Departments to organize as they please — streamed, mixed ability, etc. This, of course, enables anyone to be moved from one band to another for teaching purposes.'

25. This point was made in comments received from Ash School:

   'We realize that research limited to the third year is bound to mean that many considerations imposed by the presence of differing numbers of other pupils throughout the various schools in your sample will be ignored. One point, however, would seem to be of particular relevance — the differences in staff/pupil ratio, both between authorities and within the same authority. Our staff/pupil ratio was 0.4 below allowed establishment during 1975/76, but we are well aware of other schools within the same LEA who have been up to nine teachers over normal allocation. Needless to say, even being a modest two teachers over strength would give a degree of flexibility in curriculum planning that could falsify the true picture and make any recommendations based on that situation unrealistic in the light of the present stringent economic situation.'

26. There are of course obvious practical advantages in longer lesson units in large schools, as anyone who has stood in a busy corridor at changeover time will testify. Even with a clear passage it may take several minutes to get from one teaching area to another, or considerably longer if the school is on a split site.

27. Newsom Report (1963), p. 126.

28. Walton, J., in *The Curriculum: Research, Innovation and Change*, Edited by P.H. Taylor and J. Walton. Ward Lock Educational (1973) pp. 125–135.

29. Shaw, K.E., in *The Secondary School Timetable*, edited by Walton, J., Ward Lock Educational (1972) pp. 50–57.

30. Walton, J., in *The Curriculum: Research, Innovation and Change*, (1973) p. 128–129.

PART IV

Summary and Suggestions:
The Significance of the Framework

This book is called *Framework for the Curriculum* but in reality at least two types of framework have been discussed. In the first place, there is the outer framework of the national (and local) context of schooling — the age range of compulsory education, the types of school and for whom they are available, the level of resources provided for schools, the expectations of society about the results of schooling, the training and supply of teachers. Secondly, there is the inner framework within the school itself; the structures and systems which are set up to translate into practice the general aims of the school — in this case the curricular aims, what should be taught, studied and learned. The most obvious and detailed representation of this inner framework is the timetable itself, for as Halsall (1973) pointed out in her description of comprehensive schools, 'embedded in every school timetable is some view of what the curriculum is and what its objectives are'.[1]

But this is not the same as saying that school timetables represent the expressed aims of those who plan the curriculum. This may be the ideal, but I have suggested that in some cases the process may be reversed so that the requirements of the timetable structure can shape and even distort the aims of those who planned it. This is not intended in any sinister, Orwellian sense. I would only suggest that because the specific problems of the timetable are urgent, visible and seemingly objective, it can appear that the main task of the timetable planner is to solve these problems by moving pieces (that is pupils and teachers) around within the established framework. By contrast, achieving a consensus on the curricular questions that lie behind the timetabling process may be a difficult and long term procedure which will only yield practical solutions after much debate — for which, in school, it is so difficult to find the time.

The focus throughout has been on the 13—14 age group and their curriculum. This has involved a 'horizontal approach', taking a slice across English secondary education, and looking at all kinds of pupils in all types of school. By contrast, the bipartite 'vertical' conception of secondary education, which has for so long dominated the English scene, has often been mirrored in reviews of what is or should be the curriculum for one part of the population *or* another; grammar school *or* secondary modern school, for example. This tendency continued in major official reports till quite recently, so that the authors of the Newsom Report (1963), although anxious to start from considerations of what was right for all pupils, were constrained by their terms of reference to concentrate on half the age group — the average and below average pupils. Interestingly, the same tendency can be observed in recent planning for the new 'post-compulsory' pupils — the growing sixth-form population. Hitherto (as with grammar schools early in the century) it had only been necessary to consider the needs of a minority, for whom an academic curriculum leading to higher education seemed appropriate. Now as larger sixth forms were envisaged, open to all pupils, plans had to be made for this changing population. But when the 1968 Schools Council Working Parties on the sixth-form curriculum were set up, one took as its brief the education of those likely to enter higher education which the others considered 'the rest'.[2]

In relation to the 13–14 age group, the changes that have taken place during this century in both the outer and inner frameworks and in the curriculum itself have followed two apparently contradictory trends. On the one hand there has been a trend to move towards common patterns – secondary education for all instead of just for some, with a five year course for all, and common opportunities in – much later – a common or comprehensive school. On the other hand, there have been repeated moves to encourage diversity at the local level: the freedom for schools to introduce new subjects and for secondary modern schools to find new ways of involving their pupils in the world around them, the move from the common format of School Certificate to the more generous umbrella of GCE and later on, the CSE framework, with many examining boards developing new examinations and assessing new subjects. On the administrative front, even for the new 'common school' there was to be no one form of organization but, after 1965, many possibilities.

These contradictory trends are well illustrated, at several levels, in the issue that has come up so often in this book – the 'common curriculum'. First, this common curriculum, declared appropriate for all, seems to have grown from a particular pattern (the traditional academic) devised to engage the interest and commitment of only a minority. Secondly, even where there is a consensus about what this curriculum should contain, there may be a tension between maintaining a common course for all pupils up to the age of 14 *and* allowing some degree of differentiation. Lastly there is the contrast between the apparent simplicity of a common curriculum conceived as a common programme of subjects, and the complex reality of this programme when it is filtered through the structures of the timetable – quite apart from all the varied ways in which it may be transacted within the classroom.

How is the curriculum to be planned for the third year (or any other year)? What constraints must be borne in mind? What influences are likely to be important? Before making any comments about the third year curriculum, it is worth reviewing the changes that have taken place in the 'outer' and 'inner' frameworks of schools, and the influence these developments have had on current understanding of what constitutes a satisfactory curriculum for third year pupils.

In the outer framework, the wider context of schooling, it is fairly easy to trace the move towards establishing common patterns because it can be seen in such broad legislative and administrative measures as the successive Acts to raise the school leaving age. It is not surprising that in the period after 1902, there was a great divide between secondary and elementary schooling, because with a few brave exceptions, most elementary schools could only offer an education in the elements or basic subjects (with a little vocational preparation), even if pupils did stay on to 13+, or later. As the compulsory school leaving age was raised to 14, curricular horizons could be widened and when this became 15 (1947), it was not too difficult to persuade at least some pupils to stay for one extra year of free education,[3] thus making possible a five year course such as the secondary grammar schools (with the aid of 'free places' for scholarship pupils) had provided for many years.

But before the long awaited goal — a common leaving age of 16 — had been achieved this part of the campaign to secure common educational opportunities for all children had been somewhat overshadowed by the movement to abolish selection at 11+. If selection could be abolished, it was argued, surely this would remove the greatest obstacle to equal opportunity. It is easier to see this movement in these negative terms — against 11+ selection — than as a movement *for* the comprehensive school, because the public soon became confused as well as ambivalent about the nature and purpose of the comprehensive school. The early London comprehensive schools became the accepted model — large, mixed, 11–18 and struggling to establish themselves academically in a context where grammar schools could still claim many of the more able children in the area. Even while doubts were being expressed on many sides about whether this was what the common secondary school should be like, other versions were being tried out: junior high school/senior high school, middle school/high school, comprehensive school/sixth-form college, and the community college or campus which attempted to reach a much wider age range by serving the whole community. It is not surprising that the arguments about the merits of comprehensive education often became confused. The pressure to secure common educational opportunities for all, which had fuelled the movement to end 11+ selection (and remains directed to this end in some LEAs), began to find other outlets. Some of these were immediately controversial — for example, the pros and cons of mixed ability teaching and the need to abolish sex-bias in the curriculum — and some seemed more widely acceptable, like the importance of establishing common standards for buildings, resources and pupil–teacher ratios, and, as we have seen, the working out of an agreed 'common course' for all pupils up to the age of fourteen or so.

Meanwhile, inside many schools both old and new the framework represented by the timetable, if it had changed at all, had done so more gradually. Moreover long before the end of the bipartite system many secondary schools of all types had evolved some common ways of working. In the great majority of schools, pupils by the age of 13+ were grouped for work according to ability, with varying degrees of precision, into streams or bands. This greatly facilitated the curriculum planning process and, since all the pupils in each class could then be considered to have broadly similar needs, it was implied that this type of grouping simplified the teaching process as well. In most schools third year pupils moved in their class units from one lesson to another at regular intervals. It was true that the secondary modern schools were urged at their inception to make a fresh start in considering such basic curricular questions as what should be studied and how the work should be organized. But even while the teachers were planning new topic-centred programmes which transcended the familiar subject boundaries, the advent of the single subject GCE in 1951 made it more likely that the school would provide for the abler pupils something more akin to the familiar grammar school course. By the third year, in most cases, this course would be running within well marked subject boundaries, as a preparation for subject-orientated examination courses.

Thus when schools were amalgamated to form new, larger comprehensive schools there might not be too much difficulty in amalgamating the planning systems; the most obvious novelty might be the effects of increased size. Was it not all the more necessary to specify even more clearly than before by means of the timetable, the central planning document, exactly what group or groups a pupil belonged to and exactly what schedules should be followed, if pupils were to undertake purposeful courses suited to their ability? Certainly with the arrival of CSE courses and the move towards a five year course for the majority, the shape of the main school programme could be outlined in similar terms for all: the three year foundation course followed by two years of 'core + options', or in some cases specialized 'lines' or courses. This pattern had developed gradually since the war within the context of the five year grammar school course, and had been foreshadowed in some secondary modern schools by the provision of special or biassed courses for older pupils. In this pattern, the third year came to occupy the slightly ambivalent position between the lower and upper school which has been described earlier.

This concern to provide common educational opportunities, backed by some common understanding about how schools should be run and secondary courses planned, meant that there came to be a widely accepted view of what all pupils should study and how the work should be organized. The argument, over simplified, could be put thus: if pupils are to have common educational opportunities then it follows that none should be deprived of any subject or form of learning. Therefore all pupils should learn the same subjects, at least for several years. But since pupils differ widely in their abilities and aptitudes, they should be grouped, (for many subjects), according to their ability. In any case this is realistic, because by the age of 14 or 15 they will need to decide in what type of public examination, if any, they have the capacity to succeed.

Alongside the development of common patterns, there had also been pressure for diversity within secondary schooling. In the 'outer framework' this could be seen most clearly in the variety of secondary school types to be found in the country as a whole. Of course there had always been variety, in terms of environment, size and resources, but now a title such as 'high school' might be used for schools which differed markedly in intake, age range and expectations. Moreover, for a single school in an authority which had abandoned selection at 11+ there might be much greater diversity among the pupils themselves. Whereas a grammar school could harness all its energies to a single, short term end — ensuring for its pupils every chance of success in a basically academic programme — the school with a non-selective entry had to bear in mind the variety of needs, expectations and goals to be found among its pupil body. There was also another sort of diversity, familiar from the past and certainly not in any central plan, and that could best be seen in the 'league tables' that have been drawn up to show the resources allocated to education by different local authorities.[4] These differences could be seen in the quality of buildings and resources, the size of the pupil–teacher ratio and many other aspects of school life. And as secondary education expanded the diversity was reflected in the staffroom; young teachers from a variety of backgrounds, craft teachers who had worked in industry, older married women returning to work. Within the 'inner framework', diversity could best be seen in plans made for older pupils — the web of options schemes, leavers' courses, and provision for the members of the open sixth form. But of course there have also been many experiments in timetabling itself and in school organization, as well as the host of new curriculum projects on offer to secondary schools from the sixties onwards.

This pressure to incorporate more diversity and adapt to greater complexity began to have its effect on the familiar pattern of a third year common course, composed usually of well known subject units, and adapted to the needs of pupils by means of ability grouping. In addition to the choices that would be offered to all pupils at the end of the third year by means of option schemes, there was need for differentiation in the third year course itself. This was not only in the interest of some able pupils (who had always had the chance to specialize in languages at this age in the grammar school), it was also clearly necessary for other pupils with pressing educational needs, and might be valuable for all, so that they could have some experience of activities that would be available higher up the school — particularly, perhaps in the aesthetic/practical area. And the diversity of educational experience for the 9—13 age range, both in types of school, and in courses, methods and educational philosophies meant that in some schools pupils might be approaching a third year 'common course' with a greater variety of expectations than would be found in the more familiar 11+ entry pattern. Was it possible to develop a more flexible approach which recognized the desire of pupils of this age for differentiation, choice and diversity in the work they did, while maintaining a broad base for later learning? After all, as a Scottish educationalist said two hundred years ago, 'It is highly inexpedient, as well as unreasonable, to think of fixing down one uniform and determined scheme of education so as to oblige every individual student to learn the same thing.'[5]

It is suggested here that the subject based version of the common course for third year pupils, traced in outline in Parts II and III, is only one of several possible interpretations of the aim to provide common educational opportunities for all, an intepretation shaped by the outer and inner frameworks of schooling as it has developed during the last half century. As far as a single school is concerned, it may seem as if there is not much that can be done about the outer framework, since this is shaped by central and local government, and by other institutions which provide the resources, guidelines and constraints within which the school must work. But in English schools there is considerable freedom for the staff to decide upon and refashion the inner framework, the way in which the work of the school is organized, even redesigning the basic units from which the framework is constructed, in order to create new possibilities for teachers and pupils. It has become clear that in most secondary schools there are several types of unit used for planning work in the lower part of the school. There are subjects; there are teacher/class units of which the most familiar is a class of 27—30 pupils, (often grouped according to ability), but with several well established variants, like the half-class (mixed), the half-class (single sex) and the group of classes farmed out to a subject department for setting. Then there are time units, periods of more or less equal length, to be treated as single or multiple units; and — most intractable of all — space units, probably mostly classrooms designed to hold about 30 seated pupils, but with a variety of other spaces some intended only for specialist use as laboratories or workshops.[6]

In a stable school which has not experienced much change in its *outer* framework in recent years, units like those just described, which have been fashioned by long use, may still be the most appropriate from which to create a serviceable inner framework. In other words, it may be quite feasible to convey the intentions of those who plan the curriculum within the limits of a conventional timetable which at the same time provides some degree of flexibility for teachers working within it. It has been pointed out, for example, that 13—18 schools may have particular problems in relation to the third year curriculum simply because all the pupils are new to the school, and have arrived with a variety of educational experiences behind them. But given stable conditions and clearly defined goals, these problems can be dealt with in the framework of a conventional timetable drawn up on familiar lines.

Thus at the independent boys' selective school in our group of twenty, Cedar School, it was possible to devise a framework for this foundation year, when boys were new to the school, which was constructed of the usual units but allowed for several types of differentiation within a common course. There was differentiation by specific ability, (setting for individual subjects), and by pupil choice (choice of second foreign language and opportunities to spend additional time on art and craft subjects). But this was a boarding school with generous levels of staffing and resources, and this made it easier to build flexibility into the framework — the boundaries between curricular and extracurricular activities were less tightly drawn than in a day school — and there was more scope for adjusting the size of teaching groups to the requirements of the work in hand. The framework established by the timetable at this school seemed to be more like a permanent central building to which other pavilions and temporary structures could be added as required.

Few of these conditions obtained in the 13+ comprehensive high schools in our Stage Two sample, and, as in many other schools with a non-selective entry, there were signs that the 'inner framework' was creaking at the seams, and needed something more drastic than minor revisions of the existing pattern. Because of their particular circumstances these strains on the third year curriculum framework might be most obvious in a 13+ school. Thus while it might be generally accepted by teachers and parents that the school should provide common educational opportunities, these had to be forged quickly in a situation where the new pupils might have little common educational background. Even if there had been careful coordination of the curriculum between the contributory middle schools, and between them and the high school (a difficult and time-consuming task), there would inevitably have been differences of interpretation and style. So a one year common course in this context had to fulfil different aims from those thought out for a curriculum planned as the culmination of a three year foundation course. In these circumstances, might it not be advisable to look again at the characteristics of the timetable framework itself, and the units from which it is constructed? Perhaps the fact that there were no younger pupils in the school might contribute to new thinking about the units of time appropriate for work, as well as the possible varieties of pupil grouping. And how should the framework be adapted to express the fact that for the majority the 'third year' in this context would be the foundation of a course limited to three years?

The planning of the curriculum for a 13+ high school may indicate rather clearly the need to ask basic questions about the inner framework when the context of schooling, the outer framework, changes. This can be just as important whatever the nature of the change — for example in size, buildings or type of intake. In many cases dramatic changes of this sort can lead to prolonged discussion about the curriculum and the organizational framework of the timetable, both formally and informally. It has been suggested (Dickinson, 1975) that curriculum innovation is often directly linked to a marked change in pupil intake, and this may also be true for changes in the structure of the curriculum.[7] But it may be equally possible to adapt existing structures more gradually to meet the change, and in some ways this seems to have happened at Victoria School. In fact it may only be when the school as an institution has absorbed these changes that radical changes are likely to be made in the inner framework. Certainly it is worth remembering that it was in some of the well established comprehensive schools in our sample that moves towards a more 'open' modular timetabling system, had been made. Alternatively, an entirely new comprehensive school may provide the context for new thinking about many facets of school organization, including timetabling.

If ideas about a common third year curriculum have been partly shaped by the familiar secondary school timetabling framework, what other interpretations of this elusive concept of the common curriculum could be used to guide the planning of new structures? This was one of the tasks set for the Schools Council Working Party on the Whole Curriculum 13—16 whose conclusions were published in 1975.[8] Much of their discussion is concerned with the criteria to be used in planning the curriculum — helping teachers to ask the right questions rather than providing them with answers. So rather than making detailed recommendations about what subjects or kinds of knowledge all pupils should pursue, the authors discuss approaches to teaching, and forms of organization for the curriculum, which may provide pupils with the opportunity to 'define their interests, forge their identities and decide upon their futures.'[9] Nevertheless, in looking at prospects for the three years from 13—16, they were able to issue some clear guidelines on the shape of the curriculum to be followed by all third year pupils. The authors considered that education should provide an introduction to as many as possible of the courses likely to be available in the 14—16 stage. In order to make sensible choices, it was necessary for pupils 'to have some preliminary experience of the subjects in question. This calls for a mainly compulsory range of courses in the lower school.'[10] So while there was no prescription about exactly what should be included in this 'range of courses', once more it seemed that at third year level, balance should be achieved by ensuring that all pupils followed a common pattern, while in the fourth and fifth year the pupil could have more say in choosing a smaller number of elements that might still constitute a balanced curriculum. The Working Party wished 'to avoid any suggestion that a balanced education should be offered only to a proportion of pupils. If the concept of a balanced education has inherent merit, then the advantages it offers should be available to all pupils.'[11] This concept of 'balance' is seen to be a complex one, calling for the exercise of sensitive judgment. Should this be seen primarily as a balance of subjects, of learning styles, of time spent on different activities, of fields of knowledge or even a blend of all these and more? And should the balance be the same for all pupils of the same age?

This line of thought could be the way in to a different understanding of the idea of a common curriculum. Rather than thinking of it as a range of types of knowledge (or skills or types of activity) that should be experienced by all pupils, it may be more productive to concentrate on those types of learning which are accepted by society as essential, which pupils will not acquire elsewhere, and for which systematic long term instruction is required and, probably, some element of compulsion in order to produce long term benefits. This would seem to be the basic idea behind White's (1973)[12] concept of the 'compulsory curriculum', and he would define these essential ingredients in terms of certain types of learning which do not coincide in every case with conventional school subjects. But if a 'core curriculum' of this sort could be worked out, it might be assumed that this would absorb only part of the school's total capacity, the rest of which could be devoted to offering pupils a range of experiences for which distinctions between age groups, ability levels, curricular and extracurricular time, and between the school and other parts of the community were more flexibly interpreted. But this might require a revision of the framework for the curriculum much more radical than any considered here.

In any case it may seem irresponsible and unrealistic to talk about radical change when the atmosphere breathes retrenchment, constraint and contraction. Already predictions have been made about how lavish options schemes may have to be axed and new curriculum projects abandoned. Indeed against this background the whole idea of the common course can take on a gloomy and restrictive aspect. This is the prospect for the next few years as a Scottish headmaster saw it in January 1977:

> 'The common course will however become by the end of the year a greater reality than it is at present. When we are restricted to contract staffing a total reappraisal will be necessary, for course options at the end of S2 [cf English third year] will no longer be possible, and the common course to the end of S4 will become an economic necessity — and the grey mediocrity that that promises should give us all pause.'[13]

So according to this view the common course becomes a thing of 'grey mediocrity', a dreary uniformity enforced upon all by economic necessity. This seems too gloomy a view. Certainly all schools will soon have to face changes in their circumstances rather different in character from the 'reorganization' of recent years: declining numbers of pupils and staff, shortages of many kinds and possibly increased emphasis on performance in 'basic subjects'.

One way to meet these challenges might be to provide all schools with an 'inner framework', devised at national or regional level, and spelling out not only the subjects to be taught but where, when and how the work should be organized, thus (from one point of view) enabling teachers to get on with the task of teaching, the task for which they were trained and where their main expertise may lie.

But, even in the current atmosphere of constraint, there are many other courses open to schools and, following the argument of the last few pages, it would seem all the more important in these circumstances to employ all the talents that teachers have in order to make the best use of 'that most valuable of all educational resources — the teachers' and the pupils' time.'[14] In other words, now more than ever before as many teachers as possible should have the opportunity and the responsibility of getting involved in some aspect of curriculum planning within the school which they know best — that is, the school in which they work. And this should include some consideration of their own subject area in relation to the whole curriculum of any group of pupils, and the way this is put together in the timetable.

Reid (1975) speaks of 'the inertial forces controlling the curriculum', and considers that 'in order to deflect it [the curriculum] into a new path . . . it is necessary to devote at least as much time to the context within which the curriculum is to be implemented as to the design of the product itself.'[15] By making more teachers aware of the significance of the 'inner framework' of the school, and involving them more fully in working out some of its details a range of expertise may be built up so that this 'inner framework', and the curriculum it supports, can be more readily adapted to fit the needs of particular groups of pupils — like our third year contingent — and the changing circumstances of secondary education.

Notes

1. Halsall, E. *The Comprehensive School*, Oxford, Pergamon Press, 1973.
2. Taylor, P.H., Reid, W.A. and Holley, B.J., *The English Sixth Form: a Case Study in Curriculum Research*, London, Routledge, 1974, p. 34.
3. By the Education Act of 1944 tuition fees at maintained schools were forbidden.
4. For instance 'The elite LEAs' in *Where*, 66, Feb. 1972, and 'LEA League Table on teachers' salaries', *Where*, 75, Dec. 1972.
5. The Principal of Kings College, Aberdeen, 1760, quoted in *Times Educational Supplement*, Scotland, 14.1.77.
6. If there is great pressure on accommodation, specialist rooms may have to be used for 'classroom subjects'. This may be greatly resented by the specialist teachers concerned, who are then unable to use their 'free periods' for preparing equipment or other material that cannot be removed from the room. But this complaint may not be sympathetically heard by those teachers of 'classroom subjects' who have no 'home room' to work from.
7. Dickinson, N.B., in Reid, W.A. and Walker, Decker F., *Case Studies in Curriculum Change*, Routledge & Kegan Paul, 1975, pp 142—3. But Dickinson pointed out that innovations were often introduced only when they had been shown to be 'successful' elsewhere. He considered that in the schools he studied 'the prevalent conception was not so much the normality of accepting radical change but rather of allowing for modifications of existing structures within well-defined and familiar parameters.' (p. 178)
8. *The Whole Curriculum 13—16*, Schools Council Working Paper 53, Evans/Methuen Educational, 1975.
9. Op. cit., p. 46.
10. Op. cit., p. 48.
11. Op. cit., p. 51.
12. White, J. *Towards a Compulsory Curriculum*, London, Routledge, 1973.
13. *Times Educational Supplement*, Scotland, 14.1.77.
14. Schools Council Working Paper 53, p. 69.
15. Reid and Walker (1975), p. 252.

APPENDICES

1. The eighteen 'background studies' schools

When it had been decided that in Stage Two of the 13—14 Study more detailed inquiries than had been possible hitherto would be carried out in a much smaller number of schools than the original 110, some method had to be found of selecting this sub-sample. The research team decided to begin the process by using a well established computer-based procedure called cluster analysis.

Cluster analysis is a taxonomic procedure which has been used extensively in the zoological and botanical sciences. There are numerous methods of cluster analysis, partly because clustering techniques can be used to serve a number of different purposes, for example:

1. Finding a true typology,
2. Prediction based on groups,
3. Data exploration,
4. Hypothesis generating,
5. Data reduction.

To quote from a useful survey of the field, *Cluster Analysis* (Everitt, 1974):

'In some investigations cluster analysis methods may be used to produce groups which form the basis of a classification scheme useful in later studies for predictive purposes of some kind.'

This, roughly, is the context in which we have used cluster analysis to explore the sample of 110 secondary schools which responded to our basic information questionnaire.

Our aim was, in the first instance, to select a sub-sample of about 20 schools, which represented the whole in some empirically determined way and which could be used for Stage Two of the Project. Clearly, secondary schools can easily be grouped together — for example into boys/girls/mixed schools, or more traditionally grammar/secondary modern/comprehensive. But there are other groupings which may be important: large/small, urban/rural, for example. Using cluster analysis techniques, groupings can be established which are based on a number of variables, so that the groups should really be seen as near to or far from each other in multidimensional space. In this case 25 variables derived from the Basic Information Questionnaire were used to cover these areas:

(a) School size and type (number of pupils, number of pupils 16+, legal status, boys/girls/mixed)

(b) Resources (adequacy of playing fields, number of A/V aids, provision of curricular materials, number of laboratories and practical rooms, age of buildings)

(c) 'Eliteness' (percentage of pupils going on to sixth-form courses, percentages going to a 'dead end' job)

(d) Social cultural background (social class of pupils, linguistic/cultural problems)

(e) 'Progressiveness' (use of Mode 3, integrated courses).

From the results of the analysis* fifteen 'clusters' of schools were obtained. Some clusters were very clearly defined on easily recognizable criteria — for example 'boys' academic schools with large sixth forms' or 'large well equipped mixed city centre comprehensive schools' — other clusters were more amorphous, containing fairly large numbers of non-selective schools.

About 35 schools were selected in the first instance. Some potentially useful information was omitted from the cluster analysis because it might already have become obsolete for some schools which were undergoing reorganization. This information in an updated form was now considered — current school population, age range and type of entry for example. Care was taken that the subsample should be fairly evenly distributed geographically, so that urban/suburban and rural areas were all included. According to the size of each cluster, one, two or three schools from each were then approached to see if they would be willing to continue with Stage Two of the study. In all, eighteen schools agreed to do so. Only two small clusters were left unrepresented.

2. The two 'case study' schools

The two case study schools (both of which, of course, had been included in the cluster analysis) were selected at the same time by a different process. Certain criteria were established by the research team and their advisers, and the whole Stage One sample was inspected for schools that would meet these criteria. The first and most obvious criterion was accessibility; it was important for the sort of work envisaged for these schools that these schools should be within daily

---

* Ward's method and the Group Average method were used. These were available as part of the version of the CLUSTAN package in use in 1974 on Birmingham University's ICL 1906A computer.

travelling distance of Birmingham. It was also decided that they should be non-selective (comprehensive) schools which had been established in their present form for at least three years. As far as possible the schools should not have outstanding advantages or disadvantages in their circumstances. In all this it was hoped that the two schools would be reasonably similar, but in two respects it was thought that they should differ — in age of entry (11+ or later) and type of setting (urban/rural). Details about the two schools which agreed to take part in this aspect of the study are given on pp. 89–104.

Timetable Questionnaire (abbreviated form)

An abbreviated form of the Questionnaire is printed below, omitting response spaces, etc. Page numbers of the full version (as used in references in the text) are given in brackets.

(page 1)

1. **Distribution of Time**
   (a) What is the length in days of your third year timetable-cycle? (Is your timetable based, for example, on a 5-day cycle, a 6-day cycle, a 10-day cycle, etc.?)
   (b) How many periods are timetabled for your third year pupils in the course of one timetable-week, or 'timetable-cycle'?
   (c) In the appropriate box(es), please indicate what sort of time-units your third year timetable is based upon:

      i. Single periods of less than 50 minutes
      ii. Single periods of 50 minutes or more
      iii. Single periods of other lengths (please specify).

   (d) i. Do you make *regular* use of double periods for your third year teaching?
       ii. If *yes*, approximately what proportion of the timetable-cycle consists of double periods? (Please estimate for the whole of the 13—14 age-group).

(Page 2)

2. **Systems of pupil-grouping**
   N.B. If you organize remedial groups, please exclude these from consideration in answering this question.
   (a) Basic Teaching Groups, * Years 1—5:
   Indicate in the grid below the general form of organization used in the various age-groups.

   (Tick *one* column for each of the 5 year-groups)**

Column 1	*Column 2*	*Column 3*	*Column 4*
This year-group is not represented in this school:	The timetable for this year-group is not organized around basic teaching groups:	All basic teaching groups are drawn from the entire range of ability represented by this year-group:	Basic teaching groups are *not* drawn from the entire range of ability represented by this year-group:

   * Groups in which pupils spend 50% or more of their timetabled periods.
   ** Age Groups were 11—12, 12—13, 13—14, 14—15, 15—16.

(Page 3)
2. (b) Third year Basic Teaching Groups:
   If you have ticked either column 3 or column 4 in question 2(a), please:
   i. give brief details of your system of assigning third year pupils to basic teaching-groups,
   and ii. indicate the number and size of your third year basic teaching groups (e.g. 2 x 30, 1 x 35, etc.)

(page 4)
   (c) System of moving pupils up the school into a higher year-group:

   i. Does your school operate a system of automatic promotion to the next year-group at the end of each academic year?

   ii. If *no*, please describe briefly your school's alternative to a system of automatic annual promotion:

   iii. Roughly what percentage (if any) of the pupils *in the third year* are more than a year older or younger than the average age of their group? If more than five per cent, please give brief details.

(Page 5)
3. **Organization of the Curriculum**
   N.B. If you organize remedial groups, please exclude these from consideration in answering this question.
   (a) General outline:
   Indicate in the grid below the method of curriculum organization adopted for the various age-groups. (Tick *one* column for each of the 5 year-groups)*

Column 1	*Column 2*	*Column 3*	*Column 4*	*Column 5*
This year-group is not represented in this school:	*Every* pupil follows the same activities, though pace, balance and content may differ:	Same as Column 2, *except* that boys and girls may follow different activities in some parts of the timetable (e.g. domestic science/ handicrafts):	*All* or *some* pupils follow *one* or *two* activities not common to all (e.g. an extra language):	*All* or *some* pupils follow *three* or *more* activities not common to all:

* (Age Groups were 11–12, 12–13, 13–14, 14–15, 15–16)

Please add further comments here if you wish.

(Pages 6 and 7)

3. (b) Subjects and activities timetabled for third-year pupils: On the following two pages, please give a broad outline of your third year timetable, as explained at the head of each column. (Please continue to disregard 'Remedial' groups in this question).

(i)	(ii)	(iii)	(iv)		(v)	
Please list here all subjects and activities timetabled for third year (e.g. 'Maths', 'English', 'Form-period', 'Private Study', etc. as applicable). Please name the subjects and activities as on your timetable.	Into how many groups are pupils divided for the activity	Please indicate the number of pupils for whom this activity is timetabled. (If it is timetabled for all 3rd-year pupils please write *ALL*)	If pupils are taught in 'basic teaching-groups', please tick here	OR If pupils are re-grouped in some way, please tick here	Please indicate here the number of periods *per timetable-cycle** spent by 3rd-year pupils on each activity.	
					(a) Maximum number that any one pupil spends	(b) Minimum number that any one pupil spends
Subjects and Activities	No. of groups	Number of pupils	Tick	Tick		

* see question 1(a)

(Page 8)

3. (c) Criteria for selecting pupils to do subjects not common to all:
Where a subject is taken by *only some* of your third year
pupils (see question 3(b), col. iii), could you indicate the basis
upon which pupils were selected for the subject?

Subject(s)	*Basis for selecting pupils*

(Page 9)

(d) Criteria for regrouping in the third year:
Where you have indicated that pupils are *regrouped* for certain
activities (see question 3(b), col. iv), could you – where
possible – indicate the kind of criteria used for regrouping?
e.g. Sex of pupils might be the basis for grouping in PE
Specific ability of pupils might be the basis for grouping
in Maths
Free pupil choice might be the basis for grouping in Art &
Crafts

Subject(s)	*Basis for selecting pupils*

(Page 10)

(e) Vertical grouping:
Are any subjects or activities timetabled for your third year
pupils on a vertical-grouping basis (i.e. with third year pupils
grouped together with pupils from different year-groups)? If
yes, please give brief details of subjects and year-groups
involved.

4. **'Blocking' of Subjects on the Timetable**
Is your third year timetable deliberately arranged so that certain
subjects are scheduled for a number (or even all) of the basic
teaching-groups at the same time?
If *no*, please go on to question 5.
If *yes*, is any special use regularly made of this arrangement at
Departmental level? (e.g. use of team-teaching, rotating pupil-
groups, regular teaching of two or more groups combined, etc.)?

(Page 11)

If *yes*, please give brief details in the table below. (Please *ignore*
conventional 'setting', with fixed groups and fixed teachers).

Subject(s) 'blocked' third year	*Use made of this 'blocking'*

5. **Team Teaching**

   If your third year uses a system of team-teaching not already mentioned under 4 above, please give brief details:

(Page 12)

6. **Third Year Homework**

   (N.B. Please do *not* count private study done *in* school hours).

   (a) Are all third year pupils regularly set homework?

   (b) If *no*,

       i. Approximately how many pupils are *not* regularly set homework?

       ii. Which pupils are not set homework?

   (c) On average, how long are those pupils who are set homework expected to spend on it out of school hours *per school day*?

(Page 13)

7. **'Remedial' Teaching in the Third Year**

   Could any of the teaching in your third year be considered as 'Remedial'?

   If *no*, please go on to question 8 (page 14)

   If *yes*,

   (a) Has your school a special Department for this work?

   (b) How many of your staff are engaged principally on this work?

   (c) What procedures do you use for identifying pupils in need of special provision?

(Page 14)

   (d) Approximately how many of your third year pupils receive this special provision?

   Space given for further details, if desired.

8. **Staffing**

   (a) *Approximately* how many of your staff are aged

       over 45?

       between 30 and 45?

       under 30?

   (b) How many of your staff are men, and how many women?

   (c) *Approximately* how many of your staff have been appointed since you became Head?

   (d) For how many years have you been Head?

   (e) *Approximately* how many of your staff are non-graduates?

                              graduates?

(Page 15)
9. Work Outside the School
Please tick in the appropriate column(s) against those of the following which are *regularly* organized by the school for third year pupils

	If within timetabled hours please tick.	If outside timetabled hours please tick
3rd year Activity		
1. Fieldwork (i.e. supervised study outside school for one day or less).		
2. Residential study courses (e.g. for cultural activities, outdoor pursuits, etc.)		
3. Community-based work (e.g. helping in play-groups). Please specify.		
4. Other educational visits outside school (e.g. to theatres, museums, etc.)		
5. Please mention here any other activities taking place outside the school which are not already included above.		

(Page 16)
10. Contact with other Schools or Colleges
(a) Is any of your third year teaching *regularly* shared with staff-members of other schools or colleges?
If *yes*, please give brief details.
(b) Do any of your third year pupils *regularly* join those from other schools or colleges for any curricular or extracurricular activities?
If *yes*, please give brief details.

(Page 17)
11. Temporary Arrangements
Is your present third year timetable in any way atypical of your usual third-year timetable (e.g. because of a temporary staff shortage)?
If *yes*, please give brief details.

12. **Constraints on the Third Year Timetable**

It may perhaps be that you do not consider that your third year timetable adequately reflects the purposes and ideologies of your school.

If by any chance this is so, could you please state briefly:

i.   in which ways — in an ideal world — your third year timetable would be modified?

and ii.   what are the main constraints that hinder you from implementing the type of third year curriculum you would wish for?

(Page 18)

13. **Future Changes**

Are any important changes being actively considered for the third year timetable in 1974/75?

If *yes*, please specify very briefly.

End of Questionnaire

Note: Space for any additional comments was given.

APPENDIX C: LIST OF ABBREVIATIONS OF SCHOOL SUBJECTS

A	Art	L	Latin
		LC	Light Crafts
Bi	Biology	Lib	Library
BSc	Biological Sciences		
		M	Maths
C, Cr	Craft	MA	Mental Arithmetic
Car	Careers	Mk	Metalwork
Ch	Chemistry	Mu	Music
Civ	Civics		
Cl St	Classical Studies	Nk	Needlework
Dr	Drama	Orch	Orchestra
DSc, DS	Domestic Science		
		P, Ph	Physics
E	English	PSc	Physical Sciences
Eu St	European Studies	PE	Physical Education
EcH	Economic History		
		REL, RE,	Religious Education/
F, Fr	French	RI	Instruction
		REM	Remedial
G, Geo.	Geography	RSc, RS	Rural Science
Ge, Ger	German	RuSt	Rural Studies
Ga	Games		
G Sc,	General Science	S, Sc	Science
Gen. Sc.		Sp	Spanish
		SS, SocSt	Social Studies
H	History	Spec E	Special English
HE	Home Economics		
Hu Bi	Human Biology	TD	Technical Drawing
		TP	Tutor Period
J	Foreign languages		
	(second, third)	Wk	Woodwork

Research Advisory Group

Mr W.A. Bloomfield	: North Bromsgrove High School
Mr D. Boardman	: University of Birmingham*
Mr J. Dalton	: Whitesmore Comprehensive School, Chelmsley Wood, Birmingham
Mr R.A. Darby	: Foxford Comprehensive School, Coventry
Mr Emrys Evans	: University of Birmingham*
Mr A. Fitzgerald	: University of Birmingham*
Mrs P. Garton**	: Swanshurst Comprehensive School, Birmingham
Miss B.C. Hanks	: Mount Pleasant Comprehensive School, Birmingham
Mrs J.J. Jones	: John Willmott School, Sutton Coldfield
Mr D.R. Peters	: Hodge Hill Comprehensive School, Birmingham
Mr C. Platts	: University of Birmingham*
Mr W.A. Reid	: University of Birmingham*
Miss H.M. Roberts	: Shenley Court Comprehensive School, Birmingham
Mr M.J.W. Rogers	: Malvern College
Mr G.D. Slaughter	: Solihull School, West Midlands
Mr M. Tebbutt	: University of Birmingham*
Miss R.R. Tulloch**	: Swanshurst Comprehensive School, Birmingham
Mr J.W.R. Turner	: Alcester Grammar School, Warwickshire
Mr T. Whitehouse	: Lordswood Grammar-Technical School, Birmingham
Mr W.S. Wynne Wilson	: University of Birmingham*

Research Team :

Professor P.H. Taylor	: Director
Anne Brumfit	: Senior Research Associate (until July 1974)
Ann Hurman	: Senior Research Associate (from July 1974)
Penelope Weston	: Research Associate
Andrea Scarboro	: Research Assistant (for one year only)
Sally Ginns Irene Godfrey	: Secretaries

* Department of Curriculum and Method, Faculty of Education
** Alternating members

The Abbey School, Malvern Wells
Alexandra High School, Tipton
The Alice Ottley School, Worcester
Bablake School, Coventry
Ball Green High School, Stoke-on-Trent
Barr's Hill Grammar School, Coventry
Bewdley High School, Wribbenhall
Bishop of Hereford Blue Coat School, Hereford
The Bishop Milner R.C. School, Dudley
Bishop Ullathorne R.C. School, Coventry
Blue Coat C.E. School, Coventry
The Blue Coat School, Dudley
Blurton High School, Stoke-on-Trent
Bremand College, Coventry
Bridley Moor High School, Redditch
Brownhills High School, Tunstall
Buckpool Secondary School, Stourbridge
Caludon Castle School, Coventry
Canon Frome County School, Ledbury
Cardinal Wiseman R.C. School, Coventry
The Chantry School, Martley, Wichenford, Worcs.
The Chase High School, Malvern
Christopher Whitehead Boys School, Worcester
Christopher Whitehead Girls School, Worcester
Churchfields High School, West Bromwich
City of Coventry School, Cleobury Mortimer
The Coseley School, Bilston
Coundon Court School, Coventry
The County High School, Redditch (formerly Abbey High School)
The Crestwood School, Kingswinford (formerly Brierly Hill Grammar
    School)
The Dormston School, Sedgley
Droitwich High School
The Dudley School, Dudley (formerly Dudley Boys Grammar School,
    and now includes Dudley Girls High School, Park Boys School,
    Park Girls School)
Dyson Perrins C.E. High School, Malvern
The Earls High School, Halesowen
Edensor High School, Stoke-on-Trent
Ellerslie School, Great Malvern

The Ellowes Hall School, Lower Gornal, Dudley
Evesham High School
Fairfield High School, Peterchurch
Foxford School, Coventry
George Salter High School, West Bromwich
Grange Secondary School, Stourbridge
Hanley High School, Bucknall, Stoke-on-Trent
Harry Cheshire High School, Kidderminster
Haywood School, Hereford
Heathfield School, Kidderminster
Hereford Aylestone (Broadlands) School (formerly Hereford High
    School for Girls)
Hereford Aylestone (Widemarsh) School (formerly Hereford High
    School for Boys)
Hereford Cathedral School
The High Arcal School, Woodsetton, Dudley
High Park School, Stourbridge
The High School, Chester Road South, Kidderminster
Holden Lane High School, Sneyd Green, Stoke-on-Trent
The Holly Hall School, Dudley
Holy Trinity Convent, Kidderminster
John Willmott School, Sutton Coldfield
King Charles I Grammar School, Kidderminster
King Edward VI Grammar School, Stourbridge
Kingstone School, Hereford
The Lady Hawkins High School, Kington
Lawnside School, Great Malvern
The Leasowes High School, Halesowen
Ledbury County School
Ledbury Grammar School
The Leys High School, Redditch
Longlands School, Stourbridge
Longton High School, Stoke-on-Trent
Malvern College, Great Malvern
Malvern Girls College, Great Malvern
Menzies High School, West Bromwich
The Minster High School, Leominster
The Mons Hill School, Dudley (formerly Wrens Nest Secondary School)
North Bromsgrove High School
Nunnery Wood School, Worcester
Oldwinford Hospital School, Stourbridge
Overross School, Ross-on-Wye (formerly Ross County School)
The Pensnett School, Brierley Hill
President Kennedy School, Coventry

Prince Henry's High School, Evesham
Queen Elizabeth's Grammar School, Hartlebury
Queen Elizabeth High School, Bromyard
Ross-on-Wye School
Royal Grammar School, Worcester
Sacred Heart College, Droitwich
St. Dominic's School, Stoke-on-Trent
St. Joseph's College, Stoke-on-Trent
St. Mary's Convent, Worcester
St. Mary's R.C. High School, Lugwardine
Samuel Southall School, Worcester
The Sir Gilbert Claughton School, Dudley
South Bromsgrove High School, Bromsgrove
Sidney Stringer School and Community College, Coventry
Stanfield High School, Burslem
Stoke Park Grammar School, Coventry
Stourbridge County High School
Stourport-on-Severn High School
Stuart Bathurst R.C. High School, Wednesbury
Summerfield School for Deaf Children, Malvern
The Summerhill School, Brierley Hill
Thistley Hough High School, Stoke-on-Trent
The Thorns School, Brierley Hill (formerly Quarry Bank Secondary
    School)
Tile Hill Wood School, Coventry
Waseley Hill High School, Rubery, Birmingham
Whitecross High School, Hereford
Whitesmore Comprehensive School, Chelmsley Wood
Wigmore High School, Leominster
Willfield High School, Stoke-on-Trent
Willingsworth High School, Tipton
Wolverley High School, Kidderminster
Wood Green High School, Wednesbury
The Woodlands School, Coventry
The Woodrush High School, Hollywood, Birmingham
Woodway Park School, Coventry
Worcester College for the Blind
Worcester Girls Grammar School

REFERENCES

BENN, Caroline and SIMON, Brian. *Half Way There*, Report on the British Comprehensive School Reform, Penguin Books (second edition), 1972.

BOARD OF EDUCATION, *The Education of the Adolescent*, a Report of the Consultative Committee of the Board of Education under the chairmanship of Sir Henry Hadow, HMSO, 1926.

BOARD OF EDUCATION, Pamphlet No. 63, *Free Place Examinations*, HMSO, 1928.

BOARD OF EDUCATION, Pamphlet No. 60, *The New Prospect in Education*, HMSO, 1928.

BOARD OF EDUCATION, *Report of the Consultative Committee on the Differentiation of the Curriculum for Boys and Girls*, HMSO, 1923.

BOARD OF EDUCATION, Report of the Consultative Committee of the Board of Education on *Secondary Education with special reference to Grammar Schools and Technical High Schools*. (The Spens Report), HMSO, 1938

BOARD OF EDUCATION, Report of the Departmental Committee of *Juvenile Education after the War*. (The Lewis Report), HMSO, 1917.

BOARD OF EDUCATION Secondary Schools Examinations Council, Report of the Committee of the Secondary Schools Examination Council on *Curriculum and Examinations in Secondary Schools*. (The Norwood Report), HMSO, 1943.

CENTRAL ADVISORY COUNCIL FOR EDUCATION (England), (for the Department of Education and Science), *Half our Future* (The Newsom Report), HMSO, 1963.

CURRICULUM DEVELOPMENT ASSOCIATES, INC., *Man, A Course of Study*, (MACOS) Washington DC/Centre for Applied Research in Education, University of East Anglia, Norwich. 1968

DAVIES, T.I., *School Organisation: a new synthesis*, Pergamon Press, London 1969.

DEPARTMENT OF EDUCATION AND SCIENCE, Circular 10/65. *The Organisation of Secondary Education*, 1965.

DEPARTMENT OF EDUCATION AND SCIENCE, *Statistics of Education SS4*, Survey of the Curriculum and Deployment of Teachers (Secondary Schools) 1965—6 Part 2: The Curriculum, HMSO, 1971.

EVERITT, Brian. *Cluster Analysis*, Social Science Research Council, Heinemann Educational Books, 1974.

HALSALL, E. *The Comprehensive School*, Oxford, Pergamon Press,

1973.

HURT, John. *Education in Evolution: Church, State, Society and Popular Education, 1800–1870*, Paladin, London, 1972

INNER LONDON EDUCATION AUTHORITY *London Comprehensive Schools*, 1966.

LOUKES, Harold. *Secondary Modern*, Harrap, London 1956.

MACLURE, J.S., *Educational Documents, England and Wales*, Methuen, 1965.

MINISTRY OF EDUCATION, Pamphlet No. 1, *The Nation's Schools: their plan and purpose*. HMSO, 1945.

MINISTRY OF EDUCATION, *Secondary Education for all: a new drive*, HMSO, 1958.

MINISTRY OF EDUCATION, Secondary School Examinations Council. Committee on Secondary School Examinations other than G.C.E. Report . . . [Chairman, R. Beloe] London, HMSO, 1960.

NATIONAL UNION OF TEACHERS, *The Curriculum of the Secondary School*, 1952.

REID, W.A. AND WALKER, D.F., *Case Studies in Curriculum Change: Great Britain and the United States*, Routledge, London and Boston, 1975.

RIESMAN, D., GUSFIELD, S. AND GAMSON, Z., *Academic Values and Mass Education*, N.Y., Doubleday, 1970.

SCHOOLS COUNCIL, *The Whole Curriculum, 13–16*. Working paper 53, Evans Methuen Educational, 1975.

SIMON, Brian, *The Politics of Educational Reform 1920–1940*, (Studies in the History of Education No. I–III), Lawrence-Wishart, London, 1974.

TAWNEY, R.H., *Secondary Education for All: a new Policy for Labour*, Allen and Unwin, 1922.

TAYLOR, P.H., REID, W.A., AND HOLLEY, B.S., *The English Sixth Form: a case study in curriculum research*, London, Routledge, 1974.

TAYLOR, P.H. AND WALTON, J. (Eds.) *The Curriculum: Research, Innovation and Change*. Ward Lock Educational, 1973.

WALKER, DECKER, F., 'What Curriculum Research?', *Journal of Curriculum Studies*, 5, No. 1, 1973.

WALTON, J. (Ed), *The Secondary School Timetable*, Ward Lock Educational, 1972.

WESTBURY, Ian, 'Conventional Classrooms, "Open" Classrooms and the Technology of Teaching,' *Journal of Curriculum Studies*, 5, No. 2, 1973.

WHITE, J.P., *Towards a Compulsory Curriculum*, London, Routledge and Kegan Paul, 1973.